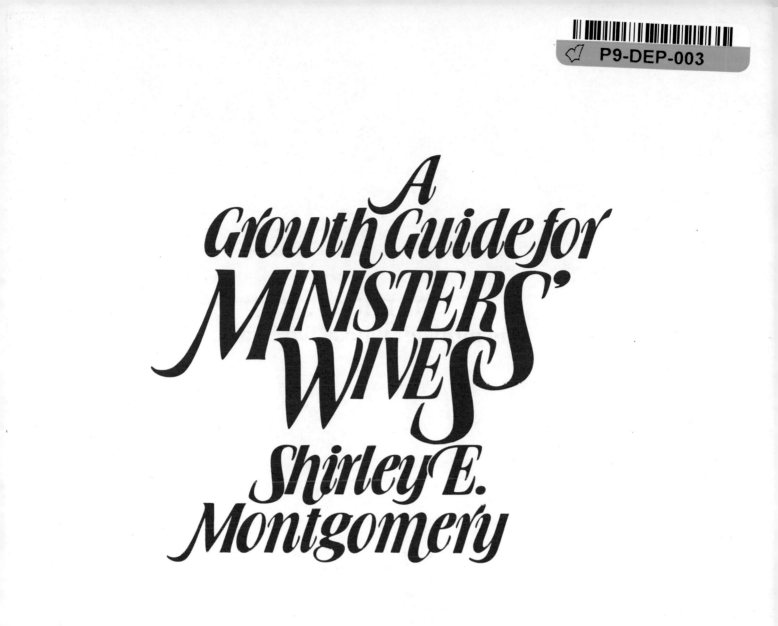

A Growth Guide for MINISTERS' WIVES

Shirley E. Montgomery

BROADMAN PRESS
Nashville, Tennessee

To Felix . . .
the minister whose wife I am.

Library of Congress Cagaloging in Publication Data

Montgomery, Shirley E.
   A growth guide for ministers' wives.

   Bibliography: p.
   I. Clergymen's wives.   I. Title.
BV4395.M58   1984   248.8'435   83-71066
ISBN 0-8054-2708-2

Contents

A Word from Wives . . .

I want to be me, not just the pastor's wife.

*I feel I am watched all the time, pressured
to do more or be better than other women.*

*I feel uncertain about myself as a minister's wife
—I'm not very open or good at sharing myself.*

How can I be myself and still be effective in ministry?

These concerns are pretty typical responses from ministers' wives as they examine their role in church life. In conferences, workshops, and wives' groups they voice their need to get in touch with their own personhood. Regardless of where they live or what type church they serve, ministers' wives share some common issues and goals: They want to be accepted as persons, and they want to be a supportive, effective part of their husbands' ministry.

If you have expressed similar concerns yourself or know someone who has, this workbook may provide some direction. Seven basic aspects of personhood have been identified and applied to the minister's wife. To help focus on these issues, a series of personal surveys or self-examination activities are set in the text. By filling in the surveys, you can draw your own profile and identify your own growth areas.

Chapter 1 gets down to the basics of who you are as a person and how this works out in what you do, how you feel, and how you react to others. Chapter 2 looks at the expectations you feel from yourself and others. Chapter 3 deals with feelings and their influence on behavior, relationships, and personal insight. Chapter 4 suggests some ways of hearing and speaking that can put you in closer touch with others. Chapter 5 examines some of the pressures of family life in the ministry. Chapter 6 offers some steps you might take in strengthening yourself and your family through the support of concerned persons around you. Chapter 7 touches at the heart of personal growth, nurturing spiritual resources. Chapter 8 provides a time of reflection, of looking back on discoveries about yourself, and of deciding what you want to do about them in the future.

As a minister's wife I often questioned my own potential to serve. I found plenty of books to tell me the ideals of being a minister's wife—what I should be doing or feeling. But I didn't find much help in seeing myself as a person or in identifying my strengths as a minister's wife. I was encouraged to find that other wives felt the same way. As other ministers' wives began to share their doubts, fears, and concerns, their love and faith began to shine through. From their struggles and mine the direction of this workbook took shape. It is my hope that as you work through this process, you too may find your faith strengthened. As ministers' wives we share a vital and redemptive outreach in our world.

1

Affirming Personhood

It is your own face that you see reflected in the water and it is your own self that you see in your heart (Prov. 27:19).

Uniqueness is a fact of human life. Like the infinite variety of snowflakes, each person is one of a kind. Similar types of personality, body shape, mental development, and such groupings can be made. But your particular combination of physical, mental, and spiritual factors is yours alone. Therefore, the logical beginning point of self-awareness is to look at the person *you* are.

Your role as a minister's wife thrusts you into the spotlight. Your personhood is drawn into fulfilling a wide range of responsibilities. You may come to view yourself more as a public figure than as a private person. You may even feel your identity as a person has been lost in the process. Ministers' wives share these feelings with wives of other high-visibility professionals: politicians, entertainers, head coaches, athletes, or public personalities in any field. You may feel, as many of these wives do, a need to express your own identity and to fulfill your own potential.

At this point many ministers' wives feel some guilt. They wonder if finding their own identity might not be a betrayal of their role. They sometimes sense a pressure to conform to popular expectations about ministers' wives rather than seek what is appropriate for themselves. It is tragic that much of the popular contemporary idea of self-expression has come to be associated with rebellion, rejection of the norm, or striking one's own path regardless of circumstances.

For Christians, however, personal growth and development of potential are included in the biblical concept of salvation and wholeness. God's grace enables us to be more of who he intended us to be. The apostle Paul spoke of personal growth as part of our heritage in the community of faith and of our ministry to one another (Eph. 4:7,13,15). He spoke of personal potential in terms of using one's gifts, being a functioning part of the body of Christ, finding oneness in faith and knowledge of Christ, and maturing spiritu-

ally according to the pattern of Christ himself. This is a far cry from "doing your own thing" or "my way—or else."

Affirming your own personhood need not be apart from or at the expense of your role as a minister's wife. Sharing in the household of faith calls for the highest development of every believer's abilities and gifts. As a minister's wife you are not exempt from this challenge, and you may sense it even more keenly.

Three major aims may be suggested in sharpening your self-awareness. First, you will want *to look at your personality and unique equipping* which you bring to your role as a minister's wife. Comparing yourself to someone else will not be of much benefit if it denies or discourages your own identity. So in this process, *your* personality will be the primary focus. Second, you will want *to identify your individual vulnerabilities and strengths* and determine how these shape your responses to daily living. You react to others out of who you are and who you perceive yourself to be. Third, you will want *to affirm your God-given worth.* This affirmation can become the basis for building a positive and redemptive life-style. Your growth toward "the measure of the stature of the fulness of Christ" will be more than a personal adventure (Eph. 4:13, KJV). Your affirmation will also touch those around you as you express God's grace in your life.

Some Basic Data About Yourself

Introducing yourself to someone involves stating some facts which place you in the context of our society. These basic outer identification marks are a good starting point in looking at your personhood. List seven things you would tell about yourself if you were meeting someone for the first time:

1. _____
2. _____
3. _____

4. _____

5. _____

6. _____

7. _____

Responses to the above list typically include name, place of residence, marital status, number of children, area of occupation for self or spouse, and other general items. On meeting strangers you tend to identify yourself by such common outward facts. You seldom reveal your more personal identity unless you feel secure in doing so.

Many aspects of your life as a woman are set in terms of roles you fulfill. Check any of the following which apply to you:

□ daughter   □ political worker
□ sister   □ denominational worker
□ wife   □ leader in your field
□ mother   □ pacesetter
□ grandmother   □ follower
□ mother-in-law   □ learner
□ friend   □ community volunteer
□ Christian   □ club member
□ church member   □ career woman
□ church worker   □ citizen

These roles represent a broad scope of relationships both in and out of your home. Were you aware of all the roles in which you find yourself? Are there other roles not listed above which apply to you? If so, list them here:

_____

_____

Meeting the Inner You

Outward identity is fairly easy to describe. Facts such as those in the preceding lists, however, are on a more public level. Your inward identity goes much deeper. How do you form an idea of who you are inside? Some of the basic sources for this kind of self-identity are:

- *Genetic factors.* These are the givens that come to you at birth: nervous system, physical appearance, inherited traits, general health pattern, intellectual capacity, innate abilities, and other inborn factors.

- *Feedback from others.* This information is made up of responses to you: how others perceive you (as good, likable, worthy, and so forth), how they value you as a person, how close they wish to be to you, how they affirm your capabilities, and how they express an opinion of you directly or indirectly. This feedback takes in how others react to you in all areas of life.

- *Role models.* Society, the entertainment media, or various groups set up ideals of popularity, success, or behavior. Measuring yourself against these ideals is part of your self-concept. You have likely selected persons you admire and would wish to be like from your childhood days onward.

- *Accumulated experiences.* This data comes from what you have observed about yourself as you go through life situations: how you react, cope, or handle events.

- *Inner sense.* Deep inside are those things which you feel about yourself and sense as real. These feelings often lie beneath the conscious level, yet influence your active thinking.

- *Successes and achievements.* This area concerns those things you do well: your accomplishments, awards, or victories—or the reverse, what you fail in.

- *Basic beliefs and values.* These factors are drawn from your religious faith, sense of commitment, and concept of right and wrong. These factors indicate how you order your priorities in life and what standard you use in doing so.

Review each of these sources of self-identity and then apply them to yourself. What specific factors have each of the sources contributed to your makeup as an individual? As you discover items about yourself, write them here:

I Have Discovered These Things About Myself as a Result of Looking at My:

Genetic factors: _____

_____

_____

Feedback from others: _____
_____
_____

Role models: _____
_____
_____

Accumulated experiences: _____
_____
_____

Inner sense: _____
_____
_____

Successes and achievements: _____
_____
_____

Basic beliefs and values: _____
_____
_____

Your concept of who you are is vital. Your self-image is the foundation of your relationship with others. You tend to see others as you see yourself. Further, your self-image is a factor in using your gifts and abilities. You may limit *what you do* by your idea of *what you can do*. Finally, your self-image is the beginning point of reaching toward your potential as a person.

To focus on your self-image, try the following exercise.

In the blanks below, list ten (10) words which describe who you are *inwardly*. Don't choose words like wife, teacher, or other more outward activities. Do choose feelings or perceptions such as *ambitious* or *intellectual*.

	1	2	3	4	5	6	7	8	9	10
1.	.	.	.	.	.	.	.	.	.	.
2.	.	.	.	.	.	.	.	.	.	.
3.	.	.	.	.	.	.	.	.	.	.
4.	.	.	.	.	.	.	.	.	.	.
5.	.	.	.	.	.	.	.	.	.	.
6.	.	.	.	.	.	.	.	.	.	.
7.	.	.	.	.	.	.	.	.	.	.
8.	.	.	.	.	.	.	.	.	.	.
9.	.	.	.	.	.	.	.	.	.	.
10.	.	.	.	.	.	.	.	.	.	.

How do you see yourself? How do you feel about what you have written about yourself? To check this out, complete the exercise by putting a small circle around the dot under the number that best expresses your feeling. The number *1* represents a *very negative* view, and *10* represents a *very positive* view. Go down the list of words and rank yourself on the scale by deciding how positive or negative each word is in describing you. When you have finished, go back to the first dot you circled and connect all ten dots down the list. When you have connected the dots you will have an attitude profile.

How did you rank yourself? Were you generally positive, negative, or neutral in your assessment? How you view yourself is a key step in the process of self-awareness. You need to have a clear, accurate, and redemptive idea of who you are. The idea must be *clear* in that it must be based on reality, not on wishes or "ought to be's." The idea needs to be *accurate* in that it reflects you truly, neither over- nor underestimating you. The idea must ultimately be *redemptive* in that it must affirm what God purposes to accomplish in you by his grace.

Checking Out Your Self-Concept

All of us have a deep need to see ourselves as individual, unique persons. When our self-concept is basically *negative*, we tend to become defensive in what we do. A lot of our energy goes into keeping up a good front. When we go to extremes in protecting ourselves from this negative view, we can turn to manipulating others, becoming withdrawn, or keeping ourselves out of activities in which we might not excel. We try to create a very safe, protected world for ourselves. We try to maintain this safe haven at all costs. Many people with very negative self-images turn to drugs or other stimulants, exhibit excesses in sexual behavior, become workaholics, or try other extreme means to feel good about themselves.

When our self-concept is basically *positive*, we are able to care, to listen, to grow, to be expressive of feelings, to be courageous, to reach toward our potential, and to be redemptive toward others. A positive self-concept builds upon our strengths yet, at the same time, does not deny or seek to disguise areas of discomfort. This positive outlook is more likely to result in a realistic approach to self and others.

If you have a basically negative view of yourself, you may need to weigh the facts to see if they support such an opinion. Your negative view may have grown out of past experiences that were not clearly understood at the time. To check out any negative view you will need to trace it back as far as possible in your memory to find its origin. This process is sometimes called "relabeling" or "replaying old tapes."

To trace the origin of a negative concept and to weigh its present value, the following questions are helpful:

1. *Why do I have this idea about myself?*

    How did I arrive at this conclusion? Is it a new idea or something from long ago? When did I begin to feel this way?

2. *Where did this idea come from—who told me so?*

    What happened to make me feel this way? Did someone tell me? Did I overhear a remark? Did I interpret someone's actions toward me as negative? Did I misread what they were saying or doing? How old was I when this first happened? What were the circumstances under which this negative view grew up?

3. *Is it right or true?*

    Do the facts bear out this idea? What evidence do I have that this view is correct? What evidence do I have that it is not true or accurate?

4. *What purpose does it serve to believe this idea?*

    Is it helpful? Does it truly show who I am? Does it serve as an excuse to keep from doing things? Do I enjoy putting myself down?

5. Does this idea continue to be true—now? *at this age? in this situation?*

    Maybe this idea was true when I was a small child, but is it true for me as an adult? Have things changed in my life so that the idea no longer fits? Does the present call for a new outlook on myself?

6. *Who am I trying to please by persisting in this idea?*

    Am I striving to be someone's ideal "little girl"? Am I trying to buy favor by accepting someone's idea of what is right for me? Am I trying to punish myself or atone for some past misbehavior? Am I trying to satisfy what I think God wants?

By sorting out our memories we can keep the good ones, toss out the bad ones, or reinterpret the bad memories to see what they mean in light of present maturity or wisdom. One minister's wife was very reluctant to sing out loud. Tracing this negative feeling back as far as she could remember, she discovered an unpleasant episode from her childhood. At about age six she visited her grandparents. As she played on the porch of their house, she sang joyously like a happy child. Her grandfather, ill and irritable at the time, heard her singing and made a few unkind remarks about all the "racket." She was crushed by this criticism and did not sing aloud again for a long time. As a child she did not understand the circumstances of her grandfather's remarks; she thought only that her singing was a bad thing. As an adult, however, she could assess this memory in its true light and free herself from its negative hold.

As adults we need to see if negative views are untruths or distortions of truth. Many adults are burdened by guilt over childhood misbehavior. Some action, particularly if it were shamed by adults, lingers like a cloud over their present lives. Many childhood experiments or high jinks are perfectly normal and natural to growing up. They should be accepted as such now and forgiven.

Stored-up negative feelings need to be replaced with a clearer understanding of ourselves. Then we need to view ourselves in light of this new truth rather than the old distortion. Whatever we may have done in the past, we surely placed it under God's grace when we gave ourselves to him. We can also surely accept his cleansing and healing now. Placing the past in God's hands redeems it and gives us a window into our lives through which we can come to understand ourselves.

If you have a particular negative feeling about yourself that lingers in your mind, write it here: _____
_____
_____

Now go back and process it to help weigh its value to you in the present:

1. Why do I have this idea about myself? _____
_____
_____
_____

2. Where did it come from? _____
_____
_____
_____

3. Is it right or true? _____
_____

4. What purpose does it serve to believe this idea? _____
_____
_____
_____

5. Does this idea continue to be true? _____
   Now? _____
   At this age? _____
   In this situation? _____
6. Who am I trying to please by continuing to hold this idea? _____
_____
_____

Gaining Self-Esteem

Self-esteem is the value you place on yourself as a person. This value follows closely on your self-concept and who you wish to be. You begin evaluating yourself by looking at people around you. You judge how they appear, behave, and get along in the world. You then decide whether you do as well, better, or worse than others. In all this process you want to think well of yourself. You are looking for self-esteem.

Self-esteem affects your thinking, emotions, behavior, relationships, desires, and goals in life. Understanding the worth you place on yourself is vital in self-awareness. A healthy appreciation for yourself is a necessary part of your growth and reaching your potential. Further, care and concern for others are rooted in the positive estimate or love you have toward yourself (Matt. 19:19).

Self-esteem is not seeing yourself as better or more important than others. Nor is it building your ego with fantasies about your appearance, abilities, popularity, or power. Rather, self-esteem is a sense of innate worth. You discover self-esteem by taking an honest, realistic, and redemptive look at yourself.

Four major areas of life experiences produce esteem, whether negative or positive.

• *Making achievements.* This area involves

succeeding at tasks, setting goals and accomplishing them, and being productive in activities.

• *Gaining influence.* When you make personal gains you sense some control over your life. From this grows a sense of having influence, having power to act, having something to say about what happens to you. This sense can come through awards, a pay raise or promotion, or recognition by others.

• *Being accepted.* This area involves a clear sense of being cared for, appreciated, and wanted. Family, friends, or significant persons in your life show interest, concern, and affection toward you.

• *Acting on beliefs.* Forming and acting on deeply held values increases a sense of personal worth. This area involves having the opportunity and feeling free to express beliefs, living by a personal standard of honor or integrity, and making a commitment to a code of behavior. Esteem is further enhanced by seeing these personal beliefs also valued by others.

Review for a moment the areas of your life which produce esteem. Check whether your sense of self-esteem is positive or negative in these areas. Also list events or feedback from others which affirm you in these areas.

My Sense of Self-Esteem

1. *Making achievements.* I feel ☐ positive ☐ negative ☐ neutral in this area.
   I feel affirmed in this area by _____
   _____
   _____
   _____

2. *Gaining influence.* I feel ☐ positive ☐ negative ☐ neutral in this area.
   I feel affirmed in this area by _____
   _____
   _____
   _____

3. *Being accepted.* I feel ☐ positive ☐ negative ☐ neutral in this area.
   I feel affirmed in this area by _____
   _____
   _____
   _____

4. *Acting on beliefs.* I feel ☐ positive ☐ negative ☐ neutral in this area.
   I feel affirmed in this area by _____
   _____
   _____
   _____

If you feel good about yourself (positive attitude) in these basic areas, you are said to have *high self-esteem.* If you feel worthless as a person or rejected by others (negative attitude), you are said to have *low self-esteem.* You probably won't always feel equally good in each area. A low in one area can usually be balanced by high esteem in other areas. However, this imbalance can be tolerated only a short time. All four areas need to be contributing at some point to produce a good sense of self-esteem.

Your sense of self-worth continues to take shape from day to day. New information about yourself keeps coming in from various sources. Present esteem is also built upon past experiences and often reflects them. Yet your self-concept can change. You can reassess your sense of worth. You can redefine your idea of who you are as a person.

Your review of your sense of self-esteem possibly indicated that you have two basic kinds of self-esteem, earned and unearned. *Earned esteem* is the kind you create through what you do: achievements gained through work or career, accomplishments, or learned skills. *Unearned esteem* is bestowed on you by others: inherited traits, social status, others' respect or attention. Both types of esteem are necessary and good. You cannot depend on just one kind of esteem. For example, you cannot gain high self-esteem purely through your achievements or work. Such an esteem would be lopsided in source and in danger of loss should you be unable to work or achieve. You need a good balance of both kinds of esteem to feel a realistic sense of worth.

Identify how you get your greatest sense of self-esteem. Review the life areas which produce esteem (p. 10) and the kinds of self-esteem. Then answer these questions:

Assessing My Self-Esteem

1. In these major areas *do I depend more* on earned or unearned esteem in order to feel good about myself:

Making achievements:	□ earned esteem	□ unearned esteem
Gaining influence:	□ earned esteem	□ unearned esteem
Being accepted:	□ earned esteem	□ unearned esteem
Acting on beliefs:	□ earned esteem	□ unearned esteem

2. From what do I gain my greatest self-esteem (appearance, work, intellect, skills, talents, income, status, or other similar factors)? _____

_____

_____

3. How permanent are these sources of esteem? How subject to change or loss are they? _____

_____

4. How would I feel about myself if I were not able to depend on this source/these sources of esteem? _____

_____

_____

5. What would balance my loss of esteem in this area of my life? _____

_____

_____

Affirming Your Self-Worth

The market is full of books that say, "If you think better about yourself, you'll be and do better." That statement is only a half truth. What you think needs to be positive, but it also must be based on reality. Your self-worth must rest on a firm foundation.

The greatest source of self-worth comes from God. His grace toward you is the foundation on which true worth as an individual is built. This source of esteem is positive and lasting. The biblical account of creation stresses three major ways in which God gave worth to every human being. First, God *made human beings in his own image* (Gen. 1:26). They shared some of his own likeness in that they were spiritual, rational beings unlike animals or other created things. God touched them with his own interactive personality so that they might be companions with him and walk with him. Second, God *gave human beings part of his own sovereignty* in caring for the earth and managing its resources (Gen. 1:28). Stewardship of the earth became humanity's first responsibility and first act of worship and obedience. Finally, God *blessed the human beings he had created* and saw that their living fulfilled his purpose (Gen. 1:28-31). Human life was good in God's sight. Sin has marred this relationship with God, but it has not removed God's intent for human beings. Their worth still lies in God's grace and in the fulfillment of his purpose in their lives.

After sin separated humans from fellowship with God, human worth was still not revoked or denied. God's plan of salvation was set into motion to restore the brokenness of persons (Eph. 1:4,10). Salvation brings wholeness to individuals, declaring their worth in God's grace. This kind of esteem is truly unearned (Eph. 2:4-5); it is bestowed on persons by right of creation and because of God's love for those whom he made.

God's gift of worth comes *just as you are*. This kind of esteem is real because God says it is true. You do not have to improve your mind, better your social position, work to attain, or punish yourself to achieve it. All that is required is an acceptance of God's love and what he has done for you. Jesus reminded his hearers that if God cared for sparrows, he certainly would care for human beings (Matt. 10:29-31).

The apostle Paul's letters to the Corinthians make clear God's gift of worth and what it can mean in your life. Three affirmations are made concerning human value. First, *you are of worth*, affirmed by the death and resurrection of Christ (2 Cor. 5:14-15). God wants persons to become what he intended for them to be. Salvation is the process by which that intention becomes reality in your life. Second, *you are a new creation* (vv. 16-18). The old rules don't have to apply forever. Life can be renewed and made fresh in God's purpose. Christ draws you to him and then gives you this great rebirth. Further, Christ makes you his messenger of this new creation so that others may find it for themselves. Third, *you are a gift* (1 Cor. 12:4-7). As a new creation, you have a job to do and a purpose in living. You have some unique place to fill in God's purpose and some personal capacity to do it. Your worth in the community of faith is affirmed by the working of the Holy Spirit in your life.

These great assurances from God in Christ should cause you to value yourself as a person of worth and purpose—just as you are. You can build on this foundation of esteem, reaching toward your potential as an individual. Accepting and trusting in God's estimate of you can pave the way for affirming other aspects of your personhood.

Reflection

1. List some things which cause you to feel good about yourself. What do you see as your most positive factors?

_____
_____
_____
_____

2. List some things in your experience which affirm you are of worth—so that you feel it, know it, sense it deeply.

_____
_____
_____
_____
_____

3. List some ways that being a new creation make you feel good about yourself as God's child.

_____
_____
_____
_____
_____

2

Defining Expectations

But the wisdom from above is pure first of all; it is also peaceful, gentle, and friendly; it is full of compassion and produces a harvest of good deeds; it is free from prejudice and hypocrisy (Jas. 3:17).

The cartoon shows a father looking through the hospital nursery window at his newborn son. The father's arms are loaded with sports equipment. This cartoon is a rather simple illustration of expectation. Expectations such as the father's dream for his son's future in athletics are fairly easy to understand. Other kinds of expectations are far more complex and less easy to pinpoint. So what are expectations and where do they come from? How do they affect you and what can be done about them?

General Expectations

Expectations can be defined as *standards of what is considered ideal, proper, or necessary.* Your life has been influenced by such standards. As you grew up you began to get an idea of what others expected of you in terms of appearance, behavior, and role in life.

Your sense of these expectations plays a very important part in your self-identity and self-esteem. For this reason you can better understand your inner direction by examining the sources and effect of expectations.

Sources of Expectations

People living or working together usually organize themselves. They adopt patterns of behavior that bring order to their shared endeavors. Over long periods of time their ideals and feelings become standardized and form the group's identity and character. Such patterns and ideals indicate certain requirements for belonging to the group and for remaining in good standing. In short, common ideas emerge which express the expectations of the group toward each other and toward outsiders they encounter.

Your experience reflects four primary sources of expectations. First, at the broadest level are *cultural expectations.* This source includes national, ethnic, and regional standards. From this type of expectation you sense what it means to be a good citizen or to be successful. Newspapers, magazines, TV, and movies showcase popular or widely admired role models in this society. Your national origin, racial or ethnic roots, and regional culture provide a particular outlook on life events and how to respond to them.

Within the broad cultural setting are *group expectations.* This source includes your local circle of associates. School, church, neighborhood, and community helped shape your ideals. You experienced "in" and "out" groups among peers. Your local standards of behavior probably guided your actions.

Family expectations form an even more basic level of ideals. The heritage of family name, status, and character gave you a certain identity. Specific individuals influenced you deeply one-on-one: parents, siblings, other relatives, and those directly involved in guiding you. The influence of your parents as role models, however, is especially crucial. Most individuals see themselves in terms of their parents' behavior. Therefore, parental responses to events and to you likely provided the cues for your own actions and attitudes.

Finally, you formed a set of *personal expectations.* You compared yourself to the ideals of culture, group, and family. From this comparison you got an idea of who and what you "ought to be." Convictions, religious commitment, moral and ethical concepts, and personal principles are also part of this process of defining your self-expectations.

Think about your formative years. Consider the kinds of expectations you sensed in growing up. What ideals or tokens of success did each of these areas hold up to you?

I. Culture: _____

_____

_____

II. Community or Local Group: _____
_____
_____
_____

III. Family: _____
_____
_____
_____

At this point it might be well to point out that your husband formed his ideals as you did. His particular background provided shaping for his concept of life-style and behavior. Your children will form their expectations from the background you are helping to shape for them.

Effects of Expectations

Understanding the process of forming ideals can give insight into how and why persons think, act, and relate as they do. Individuals tend to adopt the expectations of persons important to them. This lends great weight to social pressure and also points to problems in dealing with expectations.

Expectations have both positive and negative aspects. On the positive side expectations point to the best in what we are and do. They help us set appropriate goals and challenge us toward our potential. In this sense, expectations lead to reasonable, just, and proper behavior. Social interaction between persons is smoothed out, and shared ideals can be identified for the good of the community.

On the negative side, expectations can become rigid, unyielding standards for what is acceptable. They can take the form of unrealistic ideas about appearance, behavior, achievement, or worth. At that point expectations become burdens.

Much in our contemporary culture tilts expectations toward the negative side. Individuals feel pressured to succeed in everything—from recreation to career. Competitiveness is encouraged in almost every relationship. Beauty and sexuality are often measured as much by fantasy as by reality. People dread being out of style or out of step because of pressure to reach ideals of success and popularity.

Expectations are not always clear-cut. Finding out specific expectations can be difficult. At times they are stated directly: "People working here will observe our dress code." But just as often expectations are implied very indirectly: "Our club looks for the right kind of people." The problem comes in trying to find out who is "the right kind" of person, and if you fit the desired pattern.

Expectations carry a sense of obligation and duty. You've probably been told since childhood that you should cooperate, please others, and look attractive in public. As a result you likely want to do what is expected of you. Your behavior becomes geared toward meeting the standards of persons or groups which you consider important.

Public opinion enforces most general expectations. Society withholds approval, acceptance, or rewards from those who do not meet its standards. Loss of approval is very painful for most individuals. Therefore, desire to conform exerts great pressure. If you don't know what is expected, you may feel that you are somehow at fault. Guilt grows out of failure to comply with group standards. Further, if you adopt others' expectations without question, you may find yourself locked into a behavior pattern that does not fit your needs or personality. Energy and resources may be heavily invested in trying to meet others' standards in your life.

Consider again the negative and positive effects of expectations. Try to identify what you think others expect of you as a person. Then fill in these questions.

These Expectations of Me Have Been Very Positive, and I Feel Comfortable with Them: _____
_____
_____
_____

These Expectations of Me Have Been Very Negative, so that I Feel Guilty About Them: _____
_____
_____
_____
_____

Personal Expectations

Part of your self-identity involves deciding who you are and who you wish to be as a person. Most likely you have a mental picture of what you would like to be if you could attain all your dreams. You know how you would like to look, act, feel, and achieve. This picture can be termed your *ideal self*. Try to describe your ideal self. List seven things which show what you wish to be like or do.

I See My Ideal Self as:
1. _____
2. _____
3. _____
4. _____
5. _____
6. _____
7. _____

Along with your ideal self, you probably have an idea of your *real self*—how you actu-ally look, act, feel, and achieve. List seven things which describe your real self.

I See My Real Self as:
1. _____
2. _____
3. _____
4. _____
5. _____
6. _____
7. _____

You will want an accurate assessment of your real self. Capacities should be noted fairly, neither overblown nor underrated. Moreover, your real self and ideal self need to be in good balance. Both the ideal and the real contribute to your personality development. But neither self needs to be stressed at the expense of the other.

Look at the box in the next exercise. Locate the circle which represents your *Real Self*. Draw a circle somewhere in the box to represent your *Ideal Self* (how near or far you sense it to be from your real self). Then answer the questions.

Your estimate of how much or how little you meet expectations directly affects self-esteem. If your ideal self lies reasonably close to your real self, you can experience a sense of accomplishment and self-satisfaction. If your ideal self is too far away (too unrealistic), your real self may be left in despair. Self-esteem suffers if attainment is always beyond reach no matter how hard you strive.

Dealing with Expectations

Expectations perform a useful service. They need not be distressing even when you do not reach them. For example, the Bible contains ideals of commitment, of being God's people, and of reflecting God's holiness in the world. The aim of these expectations is not sinless perfection but rather a surrender to God's will and purpose. Maturing in your spiritual pilgrimage enables you to weigh expectations and respond to meaningful ones (Phil. 3:12-14).

Weigh expectations sensibly. Not all expectations deserve your efforts. Some demands may be based on false or trivial goals. Other demands may have grown out of a parent's

My IDEAL SELF is based on:
☐ what my parents wanted for me
☐ what I sense to be the most I can do
☐ what I think others want me to be
☐ what I sense to be right for me

I see my IDEAL SELF as:
☐ too close to be challenging
☐ about right as an ideal
☐ far enough to be frustrating
☐ too far to be realistic as a goal

ego drives. Still other expectations may appear in distorted views of Scripture or of God's will. So some practical type of test is useful in dealing with expectations.

Four keys help weigh the validity of expectations:

• *Realistic.* Expectations need to express reasonable hope of attainment. Such ideals take into account your personality, growth needs, capacities, and gifts. Expecting to be a concert pianist is not realistic if you do not have the musical capacity to do so. Therefore, test expectations for true-to-life, reasonable levels of attainment.

• *Purposeful.* Expectations should identify some worthwhile goal. Test expectations for their potential in meeting needs, providing growth, or making substantial gain in personhood.

• *Fulfilling.* Expectations should lead toward meeting your growth potential. A sense of accomplishment and worth should come from reaching toward goals. Test expectations for what they lead you to become. Ideals which deny your real self or substitute an identity far removed from your own will lead nowhere. Expectations should draw you toward excellence, but at the same time they should encourage and stimulate you in working toward them.

• *Redemptive.* For the Christian, expectations should reflect both God's call to commitment and his grace in accepting, forgiving, and redeeming persons. God does not impose standards beyond human capacity (1 Cor. 10:13; Eph. 2:4-10). Whatever you may have been is not so important as what God leads you to become. As the apostle Paul noted, "But by God's grace I am what I am, and the grace that he gave me was not without effect" (1 Cor. 15:10).

Look again at your *ideal self* (p. 15). List the seven items you chose as expectations on the lines below. Then weigh the ideals by marking the squares under each heading if you feel the expectation fits.

	Realistic	Purposeful	Fulfilling	Redemptive
1. _____	☐	☐	☐	☐
2. _____	☐	☐	☐	☐
3. _____	☐	☐	☐	☐
4. _____	☐	☐	☐	☐
5. _____	☐	☐	☐	☐
6. _____	☐	☐	☐	☐
7. _____	☐	☐	☐	☐

Role Expectations

Many expectations cluster around the various roles you play each day. A role is *a generally accepted pattern of carrying out a task or responsibility.* Some of the more basic roles relate to sex, age, marital status, work, career, religion, social activities, parenting, and community life. Certain appropriate and expected behavior patterns cling to each role.

Role expectations, much like general expectations, are also helpful. They provide part of your identity (a woman of a certain age who may be a wife and mother and who has certain responsibilities). But roles do much more. They teach how to act in various situations and identify who does what in society. This way of standardizing behavior gives stability and predictability to life.[1] For example, if you had a medical problem you would seek a doctor. A doctor's role identifies one who knows about illness and helps sick persons. You know to seek a doctor rather than a mechanic because of role identity.

Because roles are so important, you will want to have some idea of how they affect you, how to identify role stress, and how to cope with this pressure.

The Effect of Roles

Fulfilling role expectations is a very complex task. You play many roles in a day's time. Each role has its own particular responsibility and makes demands on your time, energy, resources, and capacities. Further, you are expected to function adequately in all these various roles, moving from one to the other without too much discomfort. This process calls for a great deal of skill, learning, and flexibility. Often you carry out several roles at once (mother, car pool driver, scout leader, and so on).

Look again at your checklist of roles on page 6. List your most active roles in the spaces below. Then rate yourself as to your performance level in each role:

	Performing very well	Performing adequately	Performing below par	Performing poorly
1. _____	☐	☐	☐	☐
2. _____	☐	☐	☐	☐
3. _____	☐	☐	☐	☐
4. _____	☐	☐	☐	☐
5. _____	☐	☐	☐	☐
6. _____	☐	☐	☐	☐
7. _____	☐	☐	☐	☐
8. _____	☐	☐	☐	☐
9. _____	☐	☐	☐	☐
10. _____	☐	☐	☐	☐

You probably feel good about yourself in roles which you perform well. But you may feel anxious about roles in which you feel inadequate. Difficulty in carrying out a role produces stress. The less you feel capable of success in a role, the more stress it creates. You can feel anxiety, depression, exhaustion, and physical illness from role stress. You will want to identify any pressure in carrying out your roles.

Identifying Role Stress

Role stress arises whenever you have difficulty in fulfilling a role, feel inadequate in the role, or fail to meet role expectations. Role stress can be summarized in four major categories: role conflict, role demands, role change, and role acceptance.[2]

Role conflict comes about in several ways. First, *expectations may contradict each other.* For example, you take pride in keeping a very tidy house. However, your part-time job done at home makes a big mess and requires keeping materials scattered about. Carrying out your job offends your sense of neatness. You can meet one aim but not meet both aims completely. Second, you may have *two or more roles which contradict each other.* A classic case is found in those who work outside the home and feel conflict between career and their roles as wife, mother, or church worker. Third, *your role may conflict with someone else's role.* An example might be that your activities as a church worker contradict your husband's role as a minister in the same congregation.

Role demands indicate the amount of time,

energy, ability, resources, or emotional investment a task requires. A role *may demand too much* from you. You may meet such expectations only with great difficulty or not at all. A role *may demand too little* from you. A routine, boring, or uninspiring role creates restlessness, uneasiness, or unfulfillment. Or a role *may be defined too narrowly*. The task may be so closely regulated that you cannot express yourself, use your creative abilities, or feel comfortable in your own identity.

Role change comes about when you take on a new role or drop a role. *New role* stress is common: getting married, becoming a parent for the first time, taking a new job, or the like. Uncertainty about your ability to measure up in these new roles usually occurs. *Dropping a role* also creates anxiety: being fired, retirement, loss of spouse or child, or sudden physical disability. The "empty nest" syndrome comes under this heading—a mother's sense of loss when the children are no longer at home.

Role acceptance has to do with how you feel about yourself in a particular role or how you perceive others accept you in it. You may feel unable to meet expectations, and as a result feel that others will reject or dislike you. You may fear that someone is trying to take over your role or control you in it. This kind of stress often produces anger and depression.

Go back to the list of roles you made (this page). Did you check below par or poorly in performing any roles? If so, list them in the spaces on page 19. Then try to identify what causes your feelings about the role.

Check as many boxes as apply to each role.

	Role Conflict	Role Demands	Role Change	Role Acceptance
	☐	☐	☐	☐
	☐	☐	☐	☐
	☐	☐	☐	☐
	☐	☐	☐	☐
	☐	☐	☐	☐
	☐	☐	☐	☐
	☐	☐	☐	☐

Role stress can be very subtle or even hidden. Things to watch out for: taking on too many demanding roles at one time, changing roles or taking on new ones, feeling drained by one or more roles, feeling inadequate in one or more roles, feeling rejected or punished for not measuring up in a role, fearing loss of a particular role, or feeling ill when a particular role must be carried out. These signs point to possible role stress.

Coping with Role Stress

Role stress makes for a very uncomfortable situation. You desire to get out from under the pressure. But if you are like many people, you simply accept the situation as is and try to live with it. Ignoring role stress, however, can have some bad side effects: withdrawing, self-blame, overcomplying with demands, taking feelings out on others, blaming others, denying the truth of the situation, behaving compulsively (overwork, use of alcohol or drugs, overeating, sexual promiscuity, and other extremes), or becoming physically or mentally ill.

Illness is a socially acceptable way of getting out of doing things, so many people unconsciously reduce their stress through illness. Headaches, backaches, nausea, dizziness, allergies, hypertension, colds, and ulcers are typical reactions to role stress.[3] These illnesses can come from sources other than role stress. But the absence of any obvious physical cause points up the likelihood of stress.

Handling role stress is much like dealing positively with any problem in life: pinpoint the difficulty and find possible solutions. Some questions to consider about role stress:

1. *What is the role stress?* Does pressure come from role conflict, demands, change, or acceptance? If so, locate the stress source in that particular role. For instance, if the stress comes from role demands, find out if the role is too demanding or too restricting. Or is the role very undemanding? Check out as accurately as possible the type of role stress.

2. *What would be required to eliminate the stress?* List things you would like to see happen in the role. How could the role be modified, redefined, or carried out to be more as you would like? Could you possibly drop the role?

3. *What prevents eliminating the stress?* When you see how the stress might be relieved, decide what is keeping you from doing it. Imagine the probable and possible consequences of changing, redefining, or dropping a role. Do you need more training? Do you need to understand the role better? Do you need to pinpoint others' expectations better? Are your own ideals clear or realistic about the role?

4. *What resources are needed in eliminating the stress?* Help is usually available from spouse, family, friends, professionals, and peers. Resources also include time, money, and experience in handling other roles. Who could help you understand or manage your role better? What organizations, professionals, or helping groups are available? How much time or expense would be involved? Can help be obtained conveniently? How much support and encouragement can you count on?

5. *What is the best plan of action?* Select several solutions that you feel would be helpful. Think about them from all angles, positive and negative. Then draw up specific steps to put the best plan into action. Don't generalize, "I need to think about getting help." Be specific, "On Monday I will call about joining the wives' support group." Or,

"I'll spend twenty minutes each morning planning my day."

6. *How can progress be measured?* Keep a record of what you do and the results. Also decide on a clear sign that will indicate your stress has been eliminated or reached a satisfactory tolerance level. Have some specific point in mind: a smoother relationship, an irritating factor removed, more security in the role, less fear of losing the role, or some such

recognizable achievement in coping. Review your plan of action regularly, daily if possible. What steps are going well? Do some steps need to be changed or dropped from the plan? Which steps don't work at all?

Select one of the roles in which you feel stress. Use the steps which have been suggested. See if you can find a plan of action for coping with that role's pressures.

Role: _____

1. Kind of stress (conflict, demands, change, acceptance) and also evidence that this stress is causing your feelings:
   Stress: _____   Evidence: _____
   _____
   _____

2. I think these things would help eliminate my stress in this role:
   _____
   _____
   _____

3. These things seem to be in the way of eliminating my role stress:
   _____
   _____
   _____

4. These resources will be needed in coping with my role stress:
   _____
   _____
   _____

5. These steps will help clear the way and lead to coping:
   _____
   _____
   _____

6. I can measure my progress in coping by these signs:
   _____
   _____

Role Expectations as a Minister's Wife

Being a minister's wife carries a special set of expectations. The ministry has symbolic meaning for many people. A minister serves as God's messenger and may even come to represent God for some people. Therefore, expectations and ideals are very high for those in ministry vocations. The same high ideals also embrace the minister's wife and family. Your position as a minister's wife grants a certain status which reflects many of the congregation's religious concepts. You will want to identify role expectations in this area with as much care as you give to other areas.

No exact role pattern exists for a minister's wife. Congregations tend to form their expectations of her from observation of past ministers' wives, hopes that certain needs in the church will be met by her, or on the basis of interpreting biblical passages related to women. Each congregation forms its own concept of the ideal minister's wife.

In addition to the church's concept, your husband has expectations of you—likely in terms of his own needs and aims in ministry. Finally, your sense of commitment will play an important part in how you perceive and respond to your role as a minister's wife.

Check your husband's ideals concerning

your role as his wife and your part in his ministry. He may be more comfortable if you keep a low profile as a background supporter, or he may want you to take a more active teammate role with him. He may expect you to express your own concept of service or follow his lead. Some ministers feel threatened if their wives take too active a role in the church or are perceived as an equal or better leader than themselves. Your husband's expectations will be reflected in both your shared service and marriage.

Your personal expectations as a minister's wife and your sense of commitment affect your role satisfaction. You may have come to your role with very high ideals about serving, or you may have taken on the role unsure of either its requirements or your capacities. If you are part of a two-clergy family with your own vocation in ministry, the potential for role stress is even greater. You may face a double load of demands in relation to your husband and the church. You will want to sort out your priorities and come to some tolerable balance of these expectations.

Identifying Expectations as a Minister's Wife

Begin this process by deciding how your expectations were formed. Try to recall who or what led you to believe as you do about your role. Possible sources for expectations are persons close to you, past experience in the church, examples of other ministers' wives, ideals from books or denominational publications, and your own convictions.

Focus on your role with the following survey. Begin by listing as many expectations as you can identify in each area:

The *church* expects these things of me as a minister's wife:

T O A 1. _____
T O A 2. _____
T O A 3. _____
T O A 4. _____
T O A 5. _____
T O A 6. _____
T O A 7. _____

My *husband* expects these things of me as a minister's wife:

T O A 1. _____
T O A 2. _____
T O A 3. _____
T O A 4. _____
T O A 5. _____
T O A 6. _____
T O A 7. _____

I expect these things of myself as a minister's wife:

T O A 1. _____
T O A 2. _____
T O A 3. _____
T O A 4. _____
T O A 5. _____
T O A 6. _____
T O A 7. _____

To pinpoint the source of these expectations, process your lists by choosing one of the letters at the left of each expectation. Choose *T* if you were actually *told* you were to carry out this item. Choose *O* if you *observed* other ministers' wives doing this item. Choose *A* if you *assumed* you should do this.

Those expectations which you have been *told* generally carry the most weight. You have a sense of obligation attached to these verbalized ideals. Yet those expectations which are *observed* or only *assumed* can often exert just as much influence on your behavior.

Review the keys for weighing expectations on page 17. Apply them to each of the expectations listed above.

Dealing with Expectations as a Minister's Wife

Being a minister's wife does not exempt anyone from ordinary responsibilities in marriage, parenting, or religious commitment. But resist burdening yourself with unnecessary duties that are based on wishful thinking (your own or someone else's). Many concepts about serving as a minister's wife are overly idealized and sentimentalized. These concepts need to be tested for validity in your present situation.

Seven major considerations can help assess expectations:

• *Mutual desires.* Discuss mutual expectations of family life and service with your husband. A sound relationship with him is basic to role choices. Seek an agreement on your role that is comfortable for both of you, taking into account both sets of needs and convictions.

• *Present circumstances.* Your current situation may well dictate much of your role. But circumstances may change. Use any change for more role satisfaction. On entering a new ministry field, negotiate your role. Learn what the church expects, make your preference known, and work out a mutually agreeable understanding of your role. You might have your role defined as part of your husband's call to the church. If you are already well settled, let your valid role needs be known to church leaders. Most congregations allow considerable leeway when needs are clearly understood.

• *Family needs.* The presence or absence of children can be a decisive factor in the investment of time and resources. Children's ages, health, and care needs may limit activities outside the home. Family needs vary with time, so plan to adjust your level of involvement as changes allow.

• *Economic needs.* Work outside the home may be a necessity. If so, make the church aware of limitations this places on involvement in congregational activities. Take into account the demands of full-time or part-time

employment on all your roles. If a career is optional, weigh your motives for taking a job in light of needs in other areas.

• *Personal potential.* Find out the amount of involvement you can handle without being overly stressed by role demands. Pull back from overcommitment if necessary. Select those areas which merit your efforts and give priority to them.

• *Personal commitment.* Define your sense of God's leading in your life. Then assess how fulfilling that commitment will affect your marriage, family relationships, life-style, and husband's ministry. Your service will need to be in reasonable balance with these priority concerns. Look for ways God is working in and through all your roles rather than narrowing your concept of service. Yield your expectations to the Holy Spirit and allow valid priorities to be affirmed.

• *Making the best of the present.* Removing conflicts or demands in your current role may be impossible. But try being as flexible as possible in viewing the situation. Look at the role impersonally to get a new perspective. Changing your perception of or attitude toward troublesome expectations might bring some relief. Meeting all expectations is not likely even in the best of circumstances. So hold on to essential role tasks and let lesser ones fall into their appropriate place.

If you often wish you were not a minister's wife, try keeping track of the events which trigger such feelings. A common pattern of events could be provoking the role stress. Check to see if your self-esteem is too tied up in meeting others' expectations. Yielding to others' expectations may have become an easy out rather than seeking your authentic role as a person and as a minister's wife.

Coming to love the reality of yourself frees you from too much dependence on others' ideals. The Bible challenges believers to be perfect (Matt. 5:48). Yet the biblical concept of perfection is not flawless, idealistic behavior but rather maturity and growth toward fulfilling God's purpose in your life.

Reflection

1. What expectations do you perceive God has of you?

2. What resources has God provided to help you meet his expectations?

3

Getting in Touch with Feelings

The Lord gave us mind and conscience; we cannot hide from ourselves
(Prov. 20:27).

"Feel expensive." "Feel warm and comfortable." "Feel confident." "Feel secure." These phrases from ads in a popular women's magazine show that feelings are a boon to advertisers. Feelings are potent enough to grab your attention and sell a product.

Advertisers realize that feelings are a vital part of your inner makeup, even if you don't always know their impact on your thinking. As you work through this chapter, you may come to realize the importance of feelings in your behavior, relationships, and self-esteem. You will want to understand how feelings affect you every day.

The Nature of Feelings

To help focus on feelings, read through the five statements below. Check *yes* if you believe the statement is accurate about feelings. Check *no* if you believe it is not accurate.

YES	NO	
_____	_____	1. Feelings always let you know exactly what the truth of a situation is.
_____	_____	2. Strong feelings, such as anger and fear, are sinful.
_____	_____	3. Feelings play very little part in good communication.
_____	_____	4. Strong feelings can and should be prevented.
_____	_____	5. Expressing no feelings at all is a good way of relating to others.

The exercise statements are often considered to be true. You may be surprised, however, to find they are all generally inaccurate when it comes to feelings. Feelings are helpful, needful ways of learning what goes on inside you. How feelings are *perceived* and how they are *expressed* are the important factors in understanding feelings.

Look at the following list of feelings. As you think about each feeling, complete the survey by checking one response in each of the columns.

In column A, consider what effect each feeling has on you, whether you think it is basically *negative* or *positive*. In column B, check how you accept feelings, if you think it is right (*OK*) or wrong (*not OK*) to have that feeling. In column C, mark how you feel toward expressing the emotion, if you feel *at ease* or *uneasy*.

	A EFFECT		B ACCEPTANCE		C EXPRESSION	
	Positive	Negative	OK	Not OK	At ease	Uneasy
Affection	☐	☐	☐	☐	☐	☐
Anger	☐	☐	☐	☐	☐	☐
Confidence	☐	☐	☐	☐	☐	☐
Depression	☐	☐	☐	☐	☐	☐
Disgust	☐	☐	☐	☐	☐	☐
Embarrassment	☐	☐	☐	☐	☐	☐
Excitement	☐	☐	☐	☐	☐	☐
Fear	☐	☐	☐	☐	☐	☐
Frustration	☐	☐	☐	☐	☐	☐
Gratitude	☐	☐	☐	☐	☐	☐
Guilt	☐	☐	☐	☐	☐	☐
Happiness	☐	☐	☐	☐	☐	☐
Inferiority	☐	☐	☐	☐	☐	☐

Joy	☐	☐	☐	☐	☐	☐
Loneliness	☐	☐	☐	☐	☐	☐
Sadness	☐	☐	☐	☐	☐	☐
Sensuality	☐	☐	☐	☐	☐	☐
Tiredness	☐	☐	☐	☐	☐	☐
Worry	☐	☐	☐	☐	☐	☐

Look over the list of feelings you just marked. Did you think any of them were negative or not OK? If so, see if you also felt uneasy about expressing these feelings. What feelings did you think were positive and OK to have? Do you feel more at ease expressing these? This survey helps reveal what you think about your feelings.

Feelings are intensely personal. Each feeling triggers its own emotional reaction based on your past experience. Some feelings make you happy or comfortable. Others are disturbing or not easily expressed. But all feelings indicate how you are responding inwardly to what is happening around you.

Five factors about the nature of feelings may help you understand more of what you experience.[1]

1. *Feelings are a physical reaction.* You observe what is taking place. Your body assesses the situation and prepares to act in a way that protects you. This reaction is automatic; it happens without any thought on your part. For example, you hear a sudden loud noise. Fear takes hold, and your body prepares to leave the scene if necessary. Muscles tense, heart beat increases, and breathing speeds up. These physical reactions take place in an instant to alert you in facing the situation.

Your body first reacts *physically* in all feelings. You have no control over this process, and it is both natural and normal. Emotions focus your attention on the situation at hand. Feelings such as anger, depression, and boredom are part of your body's defense system. Therefore, feelings are simply a barometer of how you are experiencing things inwardly.

2. *Feelings get expressed one way or another.* If you deny feelings, they will surface in some other form. Repressed feelings often show up as physical illness (headaches, backaches,

high blood pressure, ulcers, muscle tension, digestive and respiratory ailments, and the like). Psychological signs of mishandled feelings may be seen as anxiety, depression, irritability, nervousness, or tension.

Feelings can be denied unconsciously or deliberately. If you have been taught since childhood to show no emotion, you may have lost touch with your feelings and fail to recognize them. You may not know what you feel or misunderstand the signals. Feelings can also be deliberately suppressed in an attempt to control or hide them.

3. *Feelings are morally neutral.* Because of their physical nature, feelings are neither good nor bad in and of themselves. Experiencing any genuine emotion is not sinful. The moral implications of feelings come about in how they are interpreted and how they are outwardly expressed.

4. *Feelings are not the same as facts.* While feelings do indicate your reaction to a situation, they may not assess the event accurately. Feeling angry, for example, does not always mean the anger is justified. Letting your emotions wholly dictate your actions may not be the most reliable means of making decisions.

5. *Feelings do not have to determine your behavior.* Feelings can be identified, understood, and expressed appropriately. You may be so angry at your spouse that you could hit him with a club. But you do not have to follow through on that impulse. You *choose* what you will do. Feelings do not have to rule your responses. Further, your perception and interpretation of feelings can be changed.

Check the way you perceive feelings by completing the following exercise. Fill in the blanks after each feeling with events or situations which trigger that emotion.

These situations cause me to feel ANGRY: _____
_____
_____

I feel HAPPY when: _____
_____
_____
_____

These situations make me feel ANXIOUS: _____
_____
_____
_____

I feel GUILTY when: _____
_____
_____
_____

Were you able to pinpoint things, events, or persons that provoke the feelings in you? Your *perception* of a situation largely determines how you respond. Two people can go through the same event; one person may feel frightened, while the other may feel challenged. The difference lies in the interpretation each gives to feelings at the time.

Look again at the list of feelings on pages 24-25. Did you check any in Column B that you thought were not OK to have? If so, list them here: _____
_____
_____
_____

What about the feeling causes you to think it is not right to have? Who or what in your past led you to think this way? What do you do when you have feelings you think are not OK to have: _____
_____
_____

Strong feelings or those perceived as negative may create uneasiness. People tend to avoid such feelings if possible. Expressing emotion raises fear of losing control, breaking down in public, overreacting, or behaving foolishly. But denying or avoiding feelings only makes them more intense and frightening. Some kind of release is needed, or pressure can build up to the point of inability to express feelings meaningfully.

The Effect of Feelings

Feelings tend to create tension as they intrude into your conscious thinking.[2] This tension results in excitement, uneasiness, unrest, or discomfort. Wanting to settle these stirrings leads to some kind of action. The tension can be prolonged or brief, depending on how the feelings are interpreted and handled.

Tension is especially noticeable in stronger feelings such as anger, fear, and guilt. *Anger* comes from a sense of being threatened, thwarted, provoked, or perplexed in a situation. *Fear* also arises from threatening situations, but it can indicate being unprepared, feeling weak or inadequate, being vulnerable or dreading some urge deep within. *Guilt* generally is a sense of remorse over some wrongdoing. But guilt can also be rooted in repressed feelings, especially the ones thought to be negative.

Tension caused by feelings is not all bad. It may be a natural way of preparing yourself to face events. Certainly your body becomes more alert and sensitive to what is happening. Realistic feelings of anger and fear help you assert your own worth and take an appropriate action. All feelings give clues to your behavior, attitudes, and response to others.

Prolonged tension, however, is not desirable. Staying tense for long periods reduces physical capabilities, dims perception, and dulls feelings. Relaxing becomes difficult, and nerves stay uptight. Moreover, expressing or understanding feelings can be cut off. At this point many people resort to drugs, alcohol, medicines, or compulsive behavior in seeking some kind of relief.

A proper solution to handling feelings eliminates neither the feeling nor the tension but seeks to cope with the emotion in a wholesome way. If you cannot accept and express emotion, you will not likely feel free to relate openly to others. You may withdraw from them or misinterpret their responses to you.

Healthy, productive release from tension comes when you can confront your feelings honestly and see what is causing them. Then you can allow your feelings to help you cope with your experiences in a more appropriate way.

Review the feelings listed on pages 24-25. Did you check any that make you feel uneasy when experiencing them? If so, write them here: _____
_____
_____

What physical reactions do you have as a result of these feelings? How do you usually cope with any tension you feel? What feelings are the most difficult for you to express? ____
_____
_____
_____

Dealing with Feelings

Expressing feelings hinges on the way you interpret them and then react according to your interpretation. You likely have some well-established patterns of expressing your feelings. Focus on your responses by completing this survey:

I express *anger* by: _____
_____
_____

I express *happiness* by: _____
_____
_____

I express *fear* by: _____
_____
_____

I express *guilt* by: _____
_____
_____

I express *affection* by: _____
_____
_____

Did you have difficulty deciding how you show various feelings? People are often unaware of their way of expressing emotion. If you find this true, try to pinpoint your responses more accurately. When you identify your feelings clearly, you can cope with them better.

Feelings generally perceived as negative are often the most difficult to express. Let's look at some of the more common emotions in this category.

Anger

People usually name anger as the most intense emotion and the most troublesome

one to express. Anger is often believed to be sinful and forbidden to Christians. Yet anger at injustice, wrongdoing, threat, or perplexing events is not only natural but proper.

The Old Testament records God's anger (Pss. 30:5; 145:8; Jer. 3:12). Jesus expressed anger at some situations he encountered (Mark 3:5; 11:15). The soul-wrenching dialogues of Job pour out anger to God, complaining in bitterness and despair (Job 9:25-35). Yet God understood Job's feelings, accepted his need to express them, and answered him with grace and affirmation (Job 38—42).

The Bible does caution, "If you become

angry, do not let your anger lead you into sin, and do not stay angry all day" (Eph. 4:26), also "slow to speak and slow to become angry" (Jas. 1:19). These verses do not deny anger but do emphasize the proper, redemptive expression of it. Anger is to be acknowledged and not brooded over until it becomes an evil force to be reckoned with.

Anger can serve as a point of communication between people. Anger gets your point across—that you are upset, irritated, and the like. The challenge in expressing anger is to confront the issue in a way that leads to meaningful resolution. At times confronting the issue appropriately means venting feelings openly and loudly. At other times keeping quiet while working through anger inwardly is best. At still other times a calm, reasoned discussion is desirable. Which method to use depends on the type of anger, the situation, or the mood and understanding of the person with whom you are dealing. For example, expressing anger to a two-year-old would be considerably different than confronting your parents or employer.

Some steps in handling anger may help you decide the most appropriate method of expressing it:

• *Accepting.* Acknowledge your anger. Affirm in yourself that feeling angry is OK. Reflect on your anger and allow yourself time to calm down—the biblical advice on slowness to express anger.

• *Identifying.* What is causing you to feel angry? Is the focus of the anger in you, in someone else, in the situation, or in some force beyond your control? Seek out any underlying cause rather than going by a surface trigger. For example, you may lash out at your husband for spilling the gravy when you are actually annoyed because he was late getting in for dinner.

• *Understanding.* Is your anger based on reality? Are you facing a genuine injustice or threat, or are you getting worked up over a triviality? Is your anger directed accurately? Your anger may be within yourself due to a sense of guilt, weakness, unmet expectations, past resentments, or low self-esteem. If this is the case, any annoyance can provoke an outburst, and no rational cause for the anger will likely emerge.

Expressing honest anger is appropriate. Several clues can help spot honest anger in yourself or others.[3] First, *is the anger out of proportion to the cause?* Flying off the handle, being temperamental, or continually acting annoyed is not being honest; it is more an expression of self-centeredness. Second, *is the anger directed at persons not really involved?* Rather than confront personal responsibility, many people target scapegoats and dump on them. Some vague "they" may be given as the culprit. Third, *is anger expressed in situations which do not merit the response?* Persons sometimes become extremely outraged during sporting events or TV programs. Such overreaction may indicate pent-up anger from other sources, though stirred up by the present event. Fourth, *is anger used as a tool?* People sometimes use anger to manipulate others. They trigger negative feelings in others to make them feel anxious, guilty, or foolish. Rather than confront the angry one, people tend to back off or give in. The angry one then gains control over the person or situation. Finally, *is the anger a defense mechanism?* Persons may use anger to cover personal hurts, anxieties, or inadequacies. Aggression seems more powerful to them than allowing real feelings to surface.

• *Coping.* Look for the best way to express anger so that it is understood by those causing it or affected by it. For example, your child upsets you by wasting his school supplies. How can you get your honest feeling across to him? Without causing further strain or alienation, how can you behave toward him so that he understands the seriousness of your anger? How can you work together to change the situation? These kinds of responses are healthy means of coping with anger. Coping becomes a process of communication and healing rather than an expression of hostility or bad temper.

• *Growing.* Recurring anger episodes usually have telltale signs like a thunderstorm coming up. How can you spot these feelings as they arise? What words or situations provoke you? Can you avoid them, change your attitude, or ease the problem? Often irksome persons or events can be seen from a new perspective so they no longer appear so threatening. At times events are beyond your control and simply must be endured. Continual brooding over them results in nothing but your own misery.

Two basic human responses to threat are

known as "fight or flight" activity.[4] But neither of these responses may be particularly appropriate in most daily settings. Rather, a more effective way of coping redemptively with anger is called for. Check your typical way of handling anger by thinking of a recent anger episode. Process it through these steps:

1. Did you acknowledge your anger? Yes _____. No _____.
   If not, why? _____
   _____
   _____

2. What situation provoked your anger? _____
   _____
   _____

3. What understanding can you find about your anger?

	YES	NO	UNSURE
Was your anger based on reality?	☐	☐	☐
Was your anger directed accurately?	☐	☐	☐
Was your anger in proportion to the cause?	☐	☐	☐
Was your anger related directly to the event at hand?	☐	☐	☐
Did you use anger as a tool?	☐	☐	☐
Did you use anger as a defense?	☐	☐	☐

4. What method/s did you use to cope with the anger? _____
   _____

5. What signs will point to this kind of anger in the future?
   _____
   _____

6. What steps can you take to handle the anger appropriately if it occurs again? _____
   _____
   _____

Guilt

Guilt can be divided into two types.[5] The first type stems from sadness or remorse over a deliberate, harmful, or immoral act. Feelings of this kind are normal, reasonable, and healthy. Normal remorse carries a sense of sin, of separation from God and others, and of grief over harm done. Such feelings can lead to acceptance of responsibility, repentance, and forgiveness (Jer. 33:8; 2 Cor. 7:10).

The second type of guilt arises when a person assumes blame for something over which he or she has no control (parents' divorce, death of a loved one, or other tragic loss). Or, this kind of guilt may come from feeling worthless or unforgivable. Blame may have been carried over from childhood misbehavior or unconfessed sin. Such feelings lead to a sense of shame, failure, and despair. The person expects only punishment, rejection, or disgust from others. Such perceptions are unreasonable and unhealthy. They can lead to deep anxiety and depression. This kind of guilt is usually turned inward rather than outward as in healthy remorse.

The first step in handling guilt is to acknowledge the feeling and assess whether it is based on reality. Valid guilt comes from willfully harming someone, behaving immorally, or acting wrongfully; it has a basis in fact and can be dealt with accordingly. You can confess wrongdoing, seek forgiveness, make restitution, or do whatever is possible to mend the situation. God's grace has provided the way for sin and guilt to be removed (1 John 1:9).

Unhealthy ways to handle guilt grow out of distortions of personal worth and responsibility. You may feel if you make mistakes or fail in any part of life that all is lost. You might assume that one experience of shame must be relived all your days. You may pick out real or imagined personal flaws and continually dwell on them. You may take responsibility for every wrong thing or misbehavior that goes on around you. You can allow unhealthy guilt to rule your life: "I have this guilt feeling; therefore, I must be a horrible person." Such distortions of reality lead to a "salvation by works" attitude, the feeling that you alone can and must atone for your sins. Such an approach cuts off forgiveness and the possibility of accepting God's grace; it breaks fellowship with others.

Check your typical way of handling guilt. If you have a sense of guilt over a particular experience, process it by these steps:

1. Upon what willful action (if any) is your guilt based?
_____
_____

2. What is producing your sense of guilt? Why do you think you are guilty? _____
_____
_____

3. Assess your sense of guilt by these tests:
   YES   NO
   _____ _____ Is your sense of guilt realistic?
   _____ _____ Is it directly related to some willful act?
   _____ _____ Is it in proportion to the act?

4. What method/s did you use (confess to God and person/s involved, denial, self-condemnation, seek forgiveness, or other approaches) in handling your guilt? _____
_____
_____
_____

5. What will bring about your forgiveness? Or when will you feel forgiven? _____
_____
_____
_____

Anxiety

Anxiety is a response to any perceived threat. Fear prepares you to defend yourself. Rational, reasonable fears are good and necessary. You need to assess when you are in danger. You can expect a certain amount of anxiety from day-to-day tensions and uncertainties. Risk taking, illness of self or loved one, loss of job, and such disruptions are sources of rational fear. However, irrational fears generally grow out of less tangible sources.

Nervousness, tension, and anxiety can have a psychological basis.[6] Tension grows from inward rather than outward causes. Anxiety can come from low self-esteem. You can feel helpless, unprepared, or incapable of coping with life. Anxiety is sometimes a reaction to mishandled anger.

People tend to have negative fears about themselves in many areas of life: intelligence, social life, family life, skills and capabilities, sexuality, appearance, and power.[7] Feelings become very tender in these areas. Fears center around failing to measure up: not being as smart, popular, loving, talented, appealing, attractive, or influential as they could or should be. Personal expectations may be unrealistic, and perceived or real shortcomings take on exaggerated form.

Survey your expectations by checking the following statements. Decide how much you agree with each one as applied to yourself:

YES   NO
_____ _____ 1. If I set very high goals for myself, I should do very well.
_____ _____ 2. When I make a mistake, people think less of me.
_____ _____ 3. I should be able to solve any personal problem quickly and easily.
_____ _____ 4. If I want something really sincerely, I deserve to get it.
_____ _____ 5. There is no point in doing something if I can't do it really well.
_____ _____ 6. I can excel at anything if I try hard enough.

_____ _____ 7. Criticizing myself for failure to live up to my ideals will help me do better.
_____ _____ 8. I should not have to make the same error more than once.
_____ _____ 9. Showing weakness or behaving foolishly is a very shameful thing for me to do.
_____ _____ 10. I am less of a person if I fail at something important.
_____ _____ 11. If I do my very best at all times, people are bound to love me.
_____ _____ 12. Giving an average performance is not good enough in anything I do.

Did you agree or disagree with most of the statements? If you agreed with half or more of the statements, you have very high expectations of yourself. The higher the number of statements you accept as an approach to tasks the more you tend to be a perfectionist. Perfectionism is often accompanied by fears of disapproval, failure, or rejection.[8] Achievements must be outstanding, or the perfectionist feels incompetent and worthless. A great deal of tension and anxiety grows out of such attitudes.

Look at your fear or anxiety. What is it you fear? Why does this frighten you? Is it a reasonable fear? What can you do to remove or cope with the basis for your fear? What resources can you find to help cope with this fear?

Depression

Depression is a sense of sadness, loss, separation, or perception of loss.[9] This feeling can come from death of a loved one, divorce, loss of emotional support, breakdown of relationships, or even the fear that these events may take place. Not all depression, however, comes from real or perceived events. Some depression is caused by illness, changes in body chemistry, or reaction to medication. Depression can also come from turning anger inward rather than dealing with it appropriately.

Signs of depression are withdrawal, apathy, fatigue, hopelessness, lack of care for self, difficulty in concentrating or making decisions, and thoughts of dying or suicide. Depressed persons often feel that life is useless, that they are worthless, and that they would be better off dead.

Changes in mood, attitude, and response are natural in obvious grief and loss. People tend to work through these episodes in time and make adjustments. But some depression seems to be purely psychological in origin. Our highly mobile, competitive society may provoke some individuals to despair. Loss of

a sense of support from significant persons and groups in life may result.

Women seem more vulnerable to depression than men.[10] Women draw a great deal of self-worth from relationships with loved ones. A sense of failure or loss (whether actual or imagined) in these relationships often leads to a sense of failure in all of life. If a woman has very high expectations of herself, perceived failure in her important roles can bring on self-defeat. Feelings of helplessness and inferiority soon follow.

Handling depression is often difficult, for both energy and motivation are low. Feelings of loss need to be brought out in the open and examined. Actual losses need to be grieved over and seen as lost. Depression can be relieved in part by physical exercise, getting out with others, and becoming involved in helping others. In this way pent-up energy can be used which helps relieve the sense of loss.

Understanding depression comes about in much the same way as in other feelings. Try to pinpoint why you feel depressed. Examine your sense of worth. Are you valuable as a person only when you make high achievements or act perfectly? Or are you of worth because God loves you and has given you his grace? Reaffirm the place you fill in the lives of spouse, children, friends, and church family. Realize that if you were totally disabled, valuable ministry could still be done (prayer, encouragement, witness, and fellowship to name a few).

Affirming your potential and gifts is a step out of depression. You can build on these blessings and learn to cope with losses with the support of those who care for you.

Expressing All Feelings

You probably experience some emotions as personally positive or negative, plus some which are hard to express. Others around you do much the same in their lives. Yet all people do not experience feelings in the same way, nor do they always express them similarly. While affection may be easy for you to express openly, it might be very hard for your spouse, a parent, or a friend.

Response to feelings comes from your past experience. As in other life concerns, you likely copied ways of handling feelings from your parents or others close to you. Your spouse also developed his expression of feelings in a similar way. Of prime importance is identifying how your spouse, children, and others close to you show emotion. You will want to be aware of the signs they use to indicate various feelings: key words, tone of voice, facial expressions, gestures, and the like. Relationships can be smoothed out when you correctly read the emotion being signaled by others.

Check your skill at reading your husband's emotions. Consider the following points:

1. Feelings which my husband and I express in similar ways are:

_____

_____

_____

2. Feelings which my husband and I express differently are:

_____

_____

_____

3. I can never tell for sure when he is expressing these feelings:

_____

_____

_____

4. Expressing this feeling gives him the most difficulty:

_____

5. The feeling I wish he would show more often is:

_____

Check your answers for accuracy by discussing them with your husband. Get his feedback on different or puzzling responses. Let him tell how he expresses these feelings. Do the same for your feelings which he may misread. Help each other understand how feelings are managed. Do you need to make your feelings clearer or show more sensitivity or openness to each other's feelings?

You might want to make evaluations of your skill at reading the feelings of your children or others with whom you have close contact. Use the same suggested questions and check out the accuracy of your answers.

Feelings vary with the circumstances and people involved. Feelings you express easily to your family might be very hard to show in public or to strangers. Feelings generally believed to be positive are sometimes just as hard to handle as those thought to be negative. Affection, gratitude, joy, or confidence pose problems for many people. Feelings which are felt to be pleasant also raise fears of losing control, breaking down, overreacting, or behaving foolishly. Some individuals are no more at ease showing happy emotions than unhappy ones.

These points are important to remember in dealing with feelings:

• *Feelings are real.* What you feel is an indication of your experience in a situation, your perception of what is taking place. The feeling may be inaccurate, overreactive, or totally illogical, but that makes the feeling no less real to you. Denying or explaining away the emotion will not help and, in fact, may keep you from dealing with it.

• *Acknowledging feelings helps ease tension.* The pressure that feelings build up needs to be accepted and handled. You may not be aware of the emotions you signal by facial expressions, tone of voice, or mannerisms. If so, try to be aware of what you are feeling and why you choose to hide emotions. Accept help or encouragement in realizing and expressing your feelings.

• *Accepting feelings encourages their expression.* Try to pick up on others' feelings and let them show emotion. Before showing feelings openly, persons need some assurance they will not be criticized or rejected. Therefore, an accepting attitude is vital. You do not have to agree with the way a person feels, only accept that the feelings exist and are important to the person.

• *Expressing feelings helps deal with them.* Talking about feelings can give them a new perspective. Feelings can be compared to the situation and tested for accuracy. The real issue at hand may be uncovered. You can help someone express feelings by showing your concern and awareness of feelings: "I sense that you are [angry, anxious, worried, sad, or whatever the feeling may be] right now. If so, I'd like to know. Maybe there's some way I could help." Even if you have misread the person's feeling, he or she will clarify your impression. At least you have opened the way for sharing the feeling and

indicated your readiness to accept it.

• *Getting feelings out in the open can help control the way they are handled.* Acknowledging and accepting feelings may prevent someone from resorting to a less appropriate way of coping—withdrawal, hostility, criticism, becoming uncooperative, or taking rash action to gain a hearing.

Since feelings are so important in understanding and relating to others, expressing them appropriately is equally important. You can help in the process by accepting, identifying, and handling your emotions redemptively. Beyond this step, you can encourage others to do the same. God created persons to experience emotion. You reach out to others through feelings—empathy, compassion, and love; for these are reflections of God's grace.

Reflection

1. What feelings do you most often express to God?

What feelings do you omit when communing with God?

2. What assurances do you have that God understands *all* your feelings?

4

Listening and Communicating

Thoughtless words can wound as deeply as any sword, but wisely spoken words can heal (Prov. 12:18).

Martha and her daughter Kay have disagreed all day. Disputes came up over what Kay should wear to school, whether she could take the car, when she should do her chores, and if she could go out with friends after supper. Kay spoke very little during supper, and finally went to her room without saying good night. Martha came to the conclusion that she and Kay were just not communicating.

Communication plays a major role in most daily activities. Great emphasis is placed on the value and power of good communication in our society. To get a better idea of how communication works, let's examine some of the basic factors involved in the process.

The Nature of Communication

Communication is often taken to mean the exchange of news, ideas, or facts between persons. In its broadest sense, however, communication means any message-related behavior by one person which implies meaning to another person.[1] This concept takes in the whole range of communication, whether spoken or unspoken. Communicating is a total process of interaction between persons and not just an exchange of words.

To focus on communicating, check your responses to the following statements. Check *yes* if you feel the statement is accurate, or check *no* if you do not think so.

YES   NO

_____ _____ 1. Conflict is due to failure in communicating.

_____ _____ 2. Communicating can be improved with practice.

_____ _____ 3. Working hard enough and sincerely enough at communicating will solve problems between people.

_____ _____ 4. Failure to communicate is practically impossible.

_____ _____ 5. Communication breaks down at times, but it can be mended so it works perfectly.

_____ _____ 6. Communication takes place even if someone ignores what is said.

_____ _____ 7. Good communication means agreement.

This survey highlights some of the more common misunderstandings about communication. The even-numbered statements tend to be accurate, while the odd-numbered ones tend to be inaccurate about communicating.

Failure to communicate is rare. Communication simply means exchanging message-laden signals. As long as someone is physically or mentally able to give or receive meaning, communication can take place.[2] Saying nothing, failing to understand, ignoring the message, or disagreeing does not mean communication failed to take place. As in the example of Martha and her daughter, many sincerely felt words were exchanged without any satisfactory result. They had not

failed to communicate, only failed to agree. Even the most sincere and skillful communication cannot guarantee problems will be solved between persons or agreement reached.

If communication can't guarantee results, what can it do? For one thing, communicating is the link between persons in relationships. Needs, wants, ideas, opinions, wisdom, insight, humor, affection, and other concerns can be shared. Talking can clear the air and get facts out in the open during conflict. Understanding can grow during conversation.

Talking, listening, and exchanging ideas can accomplish much, but such activity is not a magic formula. Some realistic sense of what communication can do is needed, and some direction in how you can be more effective in the process may be helpful.

The Communication Process

Communication begins when you interpret and give meaning to sight, sound, or other sensory input. This meaning can be shared with others. How accurate the meaning may be depends on your ability to evaluate and report what happened and what you experienced in the event.

Communication involves your whole personality. Your feelings at the time, attitude toward the event or person, ability to perceive and interpret, and willingness to participate are all part of communicating. Others involved in the conversation also bring their own personalities into the exchange.

How would you describe yourself as a communicator? Check your answer by placing a circle around the letter which best describes your response to each item:

A = always

U = usually

S = sometimes

R = rarely

N = never

A	U	S	R	N	
A	U	S	R	N	1. I express my ideas clearly.
A	U	S	R	N	2. I listen carefully to others.
A	U	S	R	N	3. I ask questions if I do not understand.
A	U	S	R	N	4. I try to understand what feelings the other person is expressing.
A	U	S	R	N	5. I like to change the subject a whole lot.
A	U	S	R	N	6. I try to think up my own ideas or replies while the other person is speaking.
A	U	S	R	N	7. I like to take charge of the conversation.
A	U	S	R	N	8. I look at the person with whom I am speaking.
A	U	S	R	N	9. I feel uneasy talking with people.
A	U	S	R	N	10. I finish other people's sentences if they are slow in speaking.
A	U	S	R	N	11. I show interest in what is being said.
A	U	S	R	N	12. I check to see how the other person is reacting to my words.
A	U	S	R	N	13. I try to give my own meaning to what the other person is saying.
A	U	S	R	N	14. I try not to let what I am really thinking or feeling come through when I speak.

In describing yourself, did you mark in the *always-usually* range on questions 1 through 4? If so, you are using good habits in communicating. Marking in the *always-usually* range on questions 5 through 7, 9, 10, and 13 may indicate some difficulty in both speaking and listening.

You have a unique pattern of communicating. You will want to be aware of how this pattern affects your interaction with others. As you go through this chapter, refer to your scoring on this survey for further insight into your communication style.

Types of Communication

Communication falls into two broad types, verbal and nonverbal. *Verbal communication* uses language in some form to carry the message. Speaking and writing are the most common examples of this kind of exchange.

Nonverbal communication uses emotions and body cues to carry meaning. Facial expressions, gestures, and tone of voice are typical nonverbal cues which either carry the message or add meaning to it.

You generally use a combination of verbal and nonverbal communication. Verbal communication usually carries the main facts of a message. Nonverbal cues reveal more about feelings, self-esteem, and other aspects of your inner self. Facial expressions, for example, may be a more open response than the words you say. Even if you do not speak, your nonverbal cues may send messages to the other person about your feelings.

What type of nonverbal cues are part of your communication style? Check any cues in the following list that you use on a regular or habitual basis:

○ smiling	○ frowning	○ staring
○ raising eyebrows	○ folding arms	○ tapping fingers
○ shifting position often	○ fiddling with your clothing	○ picking at the other person's clothing
○ nodding	○ tapping foot	○ varying pitch of voice
○ touching the other person	○ changing tone of voice	○ making noise (humming, cracking knuckles, moving an object, etc.)
○ gesturing with your hands	○ keeping eye contact	
○ looking away often	○ fidgeting	
○ tilting head	○ shutting eyes	○ touching or rubbing face
○ twirling a strand of your hair	○ leaning toward other person	○ pulling at ear
	○ scratching head	

Review the nonverbal cues you checked. Do you think they are generally pleasant? Do your expressions, gestures, and body movements hint at interest or boredom when listening? Do the cues irritate or distract others? Are you relying on nonverbal cues too much to get your message across rather than saying what you feel?

Together verbal and nonverbal communication carry the message. Now let's turn to some barriers which may block the message from getting through.

Barriers to Communication

Barriers form a block somewhere in the process of communication: failure to speak, hear, understand, or respond clearly. Seven major barriers can be identified:

■ *People.* Individuals have to want to communicate. Each person must participate to some extent, make an effort, and persist in it for the process to be effective.

■ *Language.* A language different from your own might be an obvious barrier. But words in the same language can be used differently and vary in meaning from person to person. Your experience helps determine the meaning you give to words.

■ *Trust level.* What you think of the person with whom you speak is important. The greater the perceived difference between you (social, cultural, ethnic, mental, physical) the less open communication tends to be.[3]

■ *Emotions.* Feelings are a valid part of any message, but they can be expressed in a way that is distracting or confusing. Feelings also effect interpretation and response.

■ *Personal issues.* Dominating the conversation, insisting on airing personal issues, or persisting in having one's own viewpoint accepted as the only correct one are examples of shutting off the open exchange of ideas.

■ *Goals.* Each person may have a different purpose or outcome in mind for the conversation. Goals may be to sell, convince, influence, or bring about a change. These goals may be opposite or incompatible.

■ *Comprehension.* Capacity to either send or receive a message effects the process. Age, interest span, language skills, mental alertness, and physical well-being are factors that are often involved in the ability to evaluate and respond.

Barriers do exist and need to be acknowledged. All parties to the conversation will need to work together to overcome difficulties. Think of someone with whom you have problems in communicating. See if you can locate possible barriers that apply to either or both of you. Check your answers on the list.

_____ different meaning to words
_____ shyness
_____ failure to speak clearly
_____ failure to listen
_____ afraid of the other
_____ embarrassment

_____ argumentative
_____ judgmental
_____ interrupting
_____ distrust
_____ unfamiliarity
_____ getting emotional

_____ indifference
_____ talk about self too much

_____ not a good talker
_____ trying to control

Did you check any barriers that come from you? What can you do to remedy them? What barriers come from the other person? What can you do to put the person more at ease? What can you say or do that may draw you both more fully into the exchange?

Communication involves sharing something of yourself as well as sharing ideas and information. The process requires thinking, speaking, hearing, and reaching out to the other person through your personality. Look now at your style of relating to others through speaking and listening.

Communication Through Speaking

Speaking enables you to make your needs, wants, ideas, feelings, and other concerns known. You build and maintain relationships by expressing interest, affection, sympathy, encouragement, and other assurances. Communication is also vital to you as a Christian. The gospel message of redemption, forgiveness, and wholeness becomes vivid and personal as you share your faith. Effective speaking can be an outlet for your total personhood.

Consider these primary aspects of speaking. Check your ability as a communicator in each area:

1. _Effective use of words._ Speaking clearly is essential. Do you speak loudly enough to be heard? Are words spoken distinctly? Is your flow of words neither too slow nor too fast? Are your ideas presented so that others are able to follow your reasoning? Are your words appropriate to the situation and the hearer? For example, explaining something to a three-year-old would require different word choice than for an adult.

2. _Expressing feelings._ Failure to express feelings leaves others in doubt as to your needs or state of mind. What feelings do you generally express openly? Do you communicate emotions appropriately? Do you worry that others may reject or dislike you if you say what you feel?

3. _Style of speaking._ Your style involves both the sound of your voice and your manner of speaking. Does your style come across as harsh, judgmental, or domineering? Or is your manner open, accepting, and encouraging? Do you overwhelm people with the loudness of your voice? Are you courteous and considerate in sharing the opportunity to speak?

4. _Use of speech._ Do you use talk to control others or build yourself up at their expense? Examples of control are talking constantly, interrupting, changing the subject often, talking on top of others, or using a loud or strident voice. Building self up can be done by disregarding others' feelings, putting others down, criticizing, constantly correcting, or bringing up embarrassing subjects. Do you put others on the spot by fishing for compliments, pressing for answers, or asking very personal questions? Do you use speech as a weapon by withholding praise or approval when it is due? Is your speech threatening in tone?

5. _Relating to hearers._ Each person needs a certain amount of "personal space" or distance in order to feel comfortable. Some individuals do not like to be touched. Do you get too close, touch, straighten or pick at the other person's clothes, stare, or behave in too familiar a manner? Do you show respect for hearers' comfort, needs, or reaction?

Rank your style as a speaker with the following survey. Select the number you feel best describes your skill and put a circle around it for each item:

					5 = very good 1 = very poor
5	4	3	2	1	Meaning clear rather than hinted at
5	4	3	2	1	Tone of voice appropriate
5	4	3	2	1	Pitch of voice pleasant
5	4	3	2	1	Feelings expressed appropriately
5	4	3	2	1	Sensitivity to others' feelings
5	4	3	2	1	Allowing others to talk

5	4	3	2	1	Respect for others' personal space
5	4	3	2	1	Avoiding harsh, critical, or judgmental tone
5	4	3	2	1	Encouraging others to respond
5	4	3	2	1	Word choice appropriate
5	4	3	2	1	Ideas generally organized
5	4	3	2	1	Flow of words at comfortable rate

Review your scores as a speaker. What areas did you rank lowest in style? Do they center around your ability to speak or around your treatment of hearers? How do these low areas affect the message you try to get across?

You may be uncertain about your appearance, ability to speak, or having something interesting or appropriate to say. These areas can be eased by concentrating more on the other person than on yourself. Speak simply and sincerely rather than trying to impress. Accept the give and take of conversation without feeling defensive. Your sensitivity as a speaker can indicate how good a listener you will be.

Communication Through Listening

Being a good listener is one of the greatest challenges in communication. Active listening requires effort to achieve. Listening generally falls into three levels: nonhearing, hearing, and thinking.[4] *Nonhearing* means listening but not paying any attention to the person or the content of the message. *Hearing* means being involved in the exchange but quickly forgetting all that was said. *Thinking* means getting mentally involved with what is said—evaluating, analyzing, comparing, memorizing, and recalling. You don't automatically listen to others. *Listening is something you choose to do.*

Listening helps you gain from another's experience, knowledge, and insight. You can find encouragement through others' reassurances. As a listener you can help others by encouraging them to express feelings and verbalize their thoughts. Both activities help in making decisions, clarifying thinking, and releasing pent-up tension. Good listening puts the speaker at ease and often diminishes feelings of loneliness or low self-esteem.

Check your listening skills by completing the following survey. Mark your answer by placing a circle around the letter which best describes your response to each item:

A = always   R = rarely

S = sometimes

U = usually   N = never

A	U	S	R	N	1. I show interest in what is said.
A	U	S	R	N	2. I give my full attention to the speaker.
A	U	S	R	N	3. I try to guess what the speaker means.
A	U	S	R	N	4. I look at the one who is speaking.
A	U	S	R	N	5. I try to appear at ease when someone is speaking to me.
A	U	S	R	N	6. I finish sentences if the speaker is too slow in finishing.
A	U	S	R	N	7. I know what most people mean before they say anything.
A	U	S	R	N	8. I note what feelings the speaker is expressing.
A	U	S	R	N	9. I try not to interrupt the speaker.
A	U	S	R	N	10. I cut off opinions I don't like to hear.
A	U	S	R	N	11. If I am curious about the person, I ask a lot of questions.
A	U	S	R	N	12. I am easily distracted when people talk to me.

Look back over your answers. Did you mark in the *always-usually* range on questions 1, 2, 4, 8, and 9? If so, you are being more of an active listener. Did you mark in the *always-usually* range on questions 3, 6, 7, 10, and 12? If so, you may be more concerned about your own issues than in listening. Review your scores after reading the barriers to good listening given below.

Barriers tend to grow out of personal concerns that interfere with hearing the speaker. Five major barriers to active listening[5] can be identified:

■ *Wandering attention.* Inattention is often shown by asking unnecessary questions, having something repeated over and over, making remarks that have nothing to do with the topic at hand, or failing to look at the speaker. Lack of attention implies that you are bored or indifferent.

■ *Thinking own thoughts.* This practice assumes that your own ideas are more important than anything the speaker says, and that you are more interested in yourself than anything else. More attention is given to thinking up your replies than to hearing the speaker.

■ *Unwillingness to hear.* Your impression of the speaker's appearance or character may cause resistance to anything that may be said. Or you may reject any ideas contrary to your own opinions by not allowing the person to speak openly.

■ *Wishful hearing.* This practice involves glossing over the speaker's words or making up your own version of them. You take in only what you want or like to hear.

■ *Assuming meaning.* This practice means jumping to conclusions about what is said or taking the speaker for granted. You may assume you know exactly what the speaker has in mind without checking for accuracy with him or her.

Active listening is based on accepting the speaker as a person of potential and worth, even when you may disagree. This kind of listening is productive in that new perspectives can be opened up, hope shared, and resolution made possible even in conflict (Matt. 18:15-17).

Listening skills can be improved by giving more attention to the speaker. Show appreciation for the speaker's efforts at sharing. Allow the person time to speak. Pumping for information or pressing for more than the person wants to say can appear threatening. Try to be at ease. Your confidence helps relax the speaker and encourages further talk.

The way you listen and respond lets the speaker know your attitude toward him or her. Practice hearing the speaker out before injecting your own opinions. If you interrupt to persuade or argue, the speaker may withdraw. Even if you succeed in controlling the conversation, you may have lost the chance of helping any further. The point of active listening is to assist the person to clarify ideas and feel secure in speaking. Imagine how it would be if everyone used *your* listening habits as you spoke!

Communicating Feelings

You are aware of feelings in your own experience. Perhaps you have needed at times to share your joy, sorrow, or anxiety. As an effective communicator you will want to understand and allow for this need in others.

You have an advantage as a listener in that you can hear faster than the person can speak.[6] This extra time enables you to listen carefully, sense emotions, and assess what you are hearing. Since much of the speaker's meaning is implied by nonverbal cues, you can try to pick up on these signals.

Expressing feelings can be encouraged by your openness in conversation. Your attitude tends to cue the speaker's response. These steps encourage openness:

1. *Acknowledge feelings.* Don't try to deny or explain feelings away. Help get them out in the open. You might say, "I can see how this would make you upset." Or, "Sounds like you are troubled by something."

Feelings have some common signals that can be spotted.[7] *Anger* can surface as loudness, harsh language, teasing, gossip, sarcasm, or lack of cooperation in talking. *Anxiety* may appear as excessive talking, nervous laughter, secretiveness, withdrawal, avoidance, or overcautiousness. *Guilt* is sometimes revealed by self-criticism, putting self down for real or imagined wrongs, and making a lot of "I should" statements.

2. *Accept feelings without criticizing them.* People cannot help feeling a certain way; they can only control what they do about their feelings. Try not to overreact to others' emotions (or your own) which may be stirred up by the conversation. Realize that the other person may be anxious, confused, illogical, irrational, angry, or even hostile.

3. *Reflect the feelings.* When the person stops talking, recall the feelings that were expressed. Relate the feelings to the facts

mentioned, and then repeat your understanding to the person.[8] For example, your child complains to you about her new teacher, the new class rules, and her awkwardness in carrying out instructions. You might reply, "I can see you are upset. You feel overwhelmed by all the new things happening at once." Explaining your opinions, giving any advice, or offering reasons why feelings are held is not appropriate. The speaker must form his or her own ideas after hearing the feelings reflected accurately.

Listening may not change the situation. But you can help clarify the problem. You serve as a sounding board for the person to see himself or herself better. Further, your listening helps the person feel understood and accepted. Once feelings have been expressed, an appropriate response to them may be easier to work out.

How would you respond to the following episode? Go through the three steps given above, read the situation, and then choose your answers.

SITUATION: Your husband comes into the house, slams the door, and slumps down in a chair. He remarks loudly, "I really am a fool. Nobody appreciates anything I do. First the Sunday School director says he wants a training clinic for next month, and now he says he doesn't—it's not a good time. I've already ordered the materials and got two state workers lined up to teach. Who does he think he is anyway? I'd like to wring his neck!"

What feelings have been expressed (directly or implied)? _____

_____

What facts have been stated? _____

_____

What behavior (his or others) produced the feelings? _____

_____

_____

Your response: _____

_____

_____

_____

Review your answers. Did your response acknowledge feelings such as frustration, self-pity, and hostility? Did you relate the feelings to what happened? Did you reflect both the feelings and your understanding of what happened (misunderstanding about arrangements for the study course)? How could your response help the person understand better what is happening in the situation?

Building Communication

As you worked through this chapter you reviewed some of the basics of communicating. These basics need to be applied in practical ways. Marriage, family life, social interaction, and church fellowship are vital areas for clear communication.

Opening up communication with those close to you is a primary concern. You can help create a favorable environment for communication to take place. Do people who converse with you have these assurances:

YES	NO	
_____	_____	1. You can talk to me.
_____	_____	2. You can say what you feel.
_____	_____	3. You can be yourself.
_____	_____	4. You can disagree with me.
_____	_____	5. You can level with me.
_____	_____	6. You have a right to your own opinions.
_____	_____	7. You can trust me with confidential matters.

Positive responses indicate you are ready and willing for communication to take place at more than a surface level. More negative responses may mean that you are unsure of your own feelings or are reluctant to open yourself to others more than casually.

An effective communicator is willing to respond to others, accept them, and hear them out without feeling unduly threatened (fearful, anxious, defensive). If you can allow this freedom, others will have more trust in you. When mutual trust, respect, and concern are present, words can become bridges of understanding and healing.

How would you rate the climate for communication in your family? Circle the number that best describes your response to each item:

					5 = very good 1 = very poor
5	4	3	2	1	Making time for communication to take place
5	4	3	2	1	Having permission to express feelings
5	4	3	2	1	Talking things out
5	4	3	2	1	Feeling free to ask questions
5	4	3	2	1	Respecting privacy in personal issues
5	4	3	2	1	Giving praise and approval
5	4	3	2	1	Willing to confront one another
5	4	3	2	1	Hearing all sides of an issue
5	4	3	2	1	Giving encouragement
5	4	3	2	1	Keeping confidences
5	4	3	2	1	Giving each time to speak
5	4	3	2	1	Discussing problems without threats or name calling

Review your answers. What areas ranked highest? What areas ranked lowest? How can low areas be remedied? What seems to be the main barrier to having personal or family communication?

Many of the same factors which apply to family communication can also apply to social and church interaction. Go back over the family climate list above. How would your circle of friends or church fellowship rank by the same rating? What can be done to create a better atmosphere for communicating? What can you do to increase your effectiveness in these areas?

People need from each other affection, approval, encouragement, praise, understanding, sympathy, acceptance, respect, accountability, and compassion. These needs are largely filled through conversation.[9] If these needs are not acknowledged and expressed, both communication and relationships are weakened. When you have shown that you care about another's feelings and ideas, you have a better chance of making any relationship stronger and more redemptive.

Reflection

1. How do you rate yourself as a listener in relation to God?

2. What steps can you take to deepen communication in your devotional life?

   What resources can you draw upon in this process?

5

Locating Family Pressures

Homes are built on the foundation of wisdom and understanding
(Prov. 24:3).

Family life has undergone rapid change in the last few decades. Shifts in economic, social, and moral standards produced new and unexpected patterns of family structure.

Families of ministers are affected by the same trends which touch other families in the community, plus some pressures unique to those in ministry vocations. Family life for the minister is sometimes a test of Christian values in a society having very different value systems and ideals. Bringing faith to bear on family concerns becomes a clear mandate for ministers.

Identifying and coping with family pressures are essential for stability and growth. The stronger your family structure the more opportunity for personal fulfillment each member can realize. Moreover, your family's coping skills can be an encouraging example in a society often torn by loss of direction.

Identifying Family Pressures

One of the simpler ways of identifying pressure is to understand predictable life stages. While individuals differ, some common patterns of experience can be found. Each family member goes through personal stages of development and deals with that level's issues. All family members experience change and relate to one another out of those changes.

Stages in marriage, career, and aging relate to one another. What goes on in one area affects other aspects of living. For example, a disruption in career would also create tension in marriage, parenting, and personal issues.

Many reference materials are available on life stages and the problems associated with them. Howard and Charlotte Clinebell deal with marriage stages in *The Intimate Marriage* (Harper and Row, 1970). Charles William Steward outlines ministry stages in *Person and Profession: Career Development in the Ministry* (Abingdon, 1974). Bob Dale gives more detailed coverage in *Stages in a Minister's Adult*

Life Cycle (Broadman cassette). Gail Sheehy's *Passages* (Bantam Books, 1976) and Carnegie Samuel Calian's *For All Your Seasons: Biblical Directions Through Life's Passages* (John Knox Press, 1979) are popular books dealing with age development.

A summary of these stages can give you some idea of where you and your family members are now. Ministry stages are *entry* (call and preparation for entering a service field), *early ministry* (putting theology into practice, learning to be a minister), *mid-career* (reexamining goals, making decisions related to the remainder of active service, maintaining a desired level of accomplishment), *later ministry* (looking toward retirement, realizing gains and losses, coming to grips with physical limitations in serving), and *retirement* (adjusting to role loss in leaving a full-time position, looking for integrity and meaning in past service).

The marriage relationship has seven major stages: *marriage to first pregnancy* (changing from single to married role, adjusting to one another, forming the basis for a family unit), *parenting preschoolers* (learning to parent, sharing spouse with child, adjusting marital relationship to new family member/s), *parenting school children* (allowing child to find personal identity and independence, juggling career demands with family concerns and activities), *parenting teens* (conflicts over freedom and responsibility, accepting sexual maturation of teen, dealing with own aging, and keeping marital relationship vital), *children leaving home* (adjusting marital relationship after children leave, dealing with disability or death of parents, realizing unfulfilled expectations), *empty nest to retirement* (settling issues carried over from previous stage, dealing with decline in physical health or energy level), and *retirement to death of spouse* (adjusting to retirement, dealing with reality of own death or that of spouse, simplifying life-style due to health or finances, and facing the

LIFE STAGE CHART

LIFE STAGE	CURRENT STAGE	PRESSURES OR ISSUES FROM THIS STAGE
MINISTRY Husband Self (if two-clergy family)		
MARRIAGE		
PERSONAL STAGES: Husband		
Self		
Child		
Child		
Child		
Other		

future alone or dependent on others for care).

Life stages depict personal development by age divisions: *infancy* (knowing self; beginning processes of thinking, speaking, and motor coordination; learning trust), *early childhood* (connecting thought with language, increasing physical and social skills, developing independence, forming ideas of right and wrong, learning self-discipline), *childhood* (becoming independent in responsibility, initiative, personal competence, and peer relationships), *adolescence* (freedom and identity conflicts, sexual maturation, forming own sense of purpose and direction), *young adulthood* (leaving home, establishing career, choosing a mate, defining own adult imperatives), *middle adulthood* (realizing peak of career, redefining goals, "now or never" decisions about marriage and career, dealing with maturation of children, coping with unrealized expectations), *mature adulthood* (maintaining sense of usefulness, dealing with aging and death,

accepting the results of one's career and life choices).

Place yourself and members of your family on the Life Stage Chart on page 43. Choose the appropriate stage from the summaries given above. Then select issues that arise in the stage each person is experiencing. After filling out the chart, consider these questions: How do these stages relate in my family's experience? What effect does the issue in one stage produce on other areas or persons in the family? What pressure points are related to the interaction of these stages?

Ministry-related Pressures

A minister's wife and children tend to be more involved in his vocation than families of most any other career group. The traditions and expectations of ministry vary in each service field, but some common ones touch most families.[1] Check the following list for pressure points you sense for your family.

Check any answers which apply:
_____ Not enough time together as a family
_____ Inadequate finances
_____ Not enough time together as a couple
_____ Few close friends in congregation
_____ Always being an example
_____ Interruption of private time by unscheduled ministry activities
_____ Lack of privacy
_____ Conflict in church
_____ Obligation to attend more meetings or activities than desired
_____ Children singled out for attention
_____ Demands of congregation on family time
_____ Expectations of congregation
_____ Pressure to be better, more spiritual than other persons
_____ Feeling of being watched all the time
_____ Negative attitudes or criticism from church members
_____ Lack of a support group
_____ Strain from pent-up feelings or tension
_____ Lack of cooperation from church members in assuming responsibilities
_____ Other:

If your family is a typical one in ministry, pressures tend to cluster around time use, social outlets, expectations, and personal support. Such pressures are common to families who hold a highly visible public role. Further, building family identity is often diffi-

cult in the close association of a local church. You often interact socially, professionally, and economically with the same people day after day.

Put your pressure areas into perspective by answering these questions:

1. Our family experiences most pressure in these areas at the present time: _____

2. The three best things about our present ministry situation are: _____

_____

_____

_____

3. The three worst things about our present ministry situation are: _____

_____

_____

_____

4. These pressures seem to lie *within* the family: _____

_____

_____

_____

5. These pressures seem to come from the congregation or ministry field: _____

_____

_____

Try to define pressure areas as closely as possible. Then work toward pinpointing their sources. Are the congregation's expectations of your family different from your own? What family pressures arise from your own high ideals? Are ministry pressures part of an ongoing or temporary situation? Do the congregation's feelings result from experience with a former minister or his family? If so, how can this feeling be eased?

Transiency in ministry vocations often troubles families. Moving to a new ministry field uproots the social support system of family members. Outlets for personal expression have to be rebuilt. Do you fear putting down roots in a locality? How do family members deal with moving to a new location? Do you and your family close out old associations and duties in a positive way so that you feel free to take up new ones? Do you allow for a time of transition when coming to a new field?

You may feel your family's situation is fairly positive at the present. If so, concentrate on improving communication or enriching relationships. Is any family member needing extra assurance or facing more pressure than others? How can the family support this member? Are you giving direct attention to your marriage through special times with your husband, enrichment retreats, or sharing favorite interests? How does the family celebrate together? Are special events in social, school, career, or church activities acknowledged (awards, promotions, good grades, getting a driver's license, and so on)?

By now you probably have formed a picture of your family's major pressure areas.

Let's look at some general stress areas faced by families and some coping possibilities. As you proceed, look for options to apply in easing pressures.

Dealing with Pressures

Coping with family issues involves assessing causes for pressure. Once causes have been identified, plans for dealing with them need to be devised. Several areas often named by ministers' families as pressure points are: time use, social outlets, and expectations. Another often named concern, personal support, will be covered in chapter 6.

Time Use

You control the use of your time. But do you know how your time is invested in various activities? To get an idea of your typical schedule, list everything you do in a week. Be sure to include each 24-hour period (sleeping, eating, personal care, household tasks, workday if employed, social outings, church activities, rest, hobbies, child care, time with husband, time with children, family outings, watching TV, reading or studying, devotional activities, shopping, club or civic involvement, travel, plus any other items in your routine). List *what you ordinarily do*, not exceptional activities during vacations or holidays.

Use your completed list to place priorities on activities. Fill out the Time Use Chart on page 46. Rank each activity by listing it under one of these headings: *Essential* (absolutely must be done), *Important* (fairly necessary), *Helpful* (nice but not necessary), *Trivial* (unnecessary).

TIME USE CHART

Priority Rankings			
ESSENTIAL	**IMPORTANT**	**HELPFUL**	**TRIVIAL**
Activity:	Activity:	Activity:	Activity:

After listing activities in the columns, estimate how much time is spent in a week on each activity and write it by the item. Put your time use in perspective by assessing the value, quality, or fulfillment each activity adds. Often less glamorous activities are very valuable, though perhaps not as inspiring or challenging as other tasks. How much time falls under *Helpful* or *Trivial* headings? How many of these activities can be dropped altogether from your schedule? Check to see if you listed necessary recreation or rest under the lowest priority heading. If so, you may wish to review your priorities again.

Consider your approach to activities. Do you plan time use? Do you put off necessary tasks? Do you think through tasks, organizing what you will need to complete them? Do you expect to accomplish too many tasks in a day? Do you allow sufficient time for tasks so that you don't have to work under pressure? If you feel undue pressure from activities, try eliminating less necessary tasks rather than struggling to complete them all.

Consider your skill in carrying out necessary tasks. Do you work efficiently? Are better or simpler methods available? Can you delegate or share some of these tasks? Do you need more training in some tasks? If so, where can you get it?

Select one or two ways you might use in making your time use more productive. Try them out for a week. Then evaluate the results. Were you more effective in what you did? Did you finish tasks with less strain?

See if you can find a comfortable pace for completing necessary tasks. When these tasks are done first and more effectively, you will feel less pressured. You may also find your time use more flexible in meeting those unexpected events which add so much color and character to life.

Social Outlets

Your family may be involved in a good many activities. However, casual outings and relaxation apart from church or other highly organized groups may be limited. Activities with church members are valuable and necessary when your husband serves a local congregation. Yet such activities often fail to produce close, accepting relationships. That is, family members may continually feel "on the spot" when placed in a leadership role or status during activities.

Check the social climate of your family by completing the following survey. Rank statements by circling a number by the item which best reflects your feeling:

5 = always 4 = usually 3 = sometimes 2 = rarely 1 = never

5	4	3	2	1	We have close friends outside our ministry field or local church.
5	4	3	2	1	Our family plans recreational activities separate from those which are part of ministry responsibilities.
5	4	3	2	1	Our children see adult role models in a wide range of social events.
5	4	3	2	1	Family members have friends with whom they can share confidences and be themselves.
5	4	3	2	1	Family members are encouraged to develop personal interests, hobbies, or play activities.
5	4	3	2	1	Family members have free time outside of organized church, club, school, or sports settings.
5	4	3	2	1	Our children have opportunity to relate to persons of varying ages and interests.
5	4	3	2	1	Family members enjoy spontaneous play meant for fun more than competition.

Review your answers. Did you mark in the *always-usually* range on most questions? If so, you likely enjoy a sense of release from routine. Lower scoring might indicate your family is locked into a routine or a narrow circle of associates. Family members can feel isolated if their only activities are in highly organized group settings.

Your family can experience release from pressure through social interaction with accepting, understanding friends. Providing breaks in daily routines can also help cope with change and bring a joyful sense of anticipation. Moreover, social relationships help persons be more responsive and open to others in all areas of life. Jesus provided times of rest for his disciples and knew the wisdom of that release (Mark 6:31).

Expectations

Children of ministers can experience considerable emotional and social pressure. They move in two worlds—inside and outside the church. Expectations from these two spheres may compete or collide. When conflicting expectations get too numerous, ministers' children sometimes "drop out" or rebel. They may choose disruptive behavior just to show they are "normal" or free to be like others their age.

Children of ministers are usually brought up with high ideals of morality and behavior. They are often given high expectations of the church and of church members. These children can grow bitter or disillusioned when church members fail to meet these ideals. They may withdraw from the church or reject the teachings or religious practices of their parents.

Children of ministers may also be victims of their parents' service zeal. Parents may be so busy in ministry activities that they neglect their children's needs. Another aspect of this problem arises when ministry couples accept the idea that their children *should* be better, never misbehaving or erring in any way. The child's capacities, gifts, personality, or vulnerabilities may be ignored in order to mold a "perfect" child. Some parents restrict their children's actions so closely that they never "leave home" emotionally.[2]

Review the expectations your children face by checking the answers on the following survey. Choose the response that most nearly describes your feeling:

YES	NO	SOME-TIME	
_____	_____	_____	Our child/children:
_____	_____	_____	1. Understand the basic moral and spiritual values by which our family seeks to live.
_____	_____	_____	2. Are expected to take the lead in all church activities in their age groups.
_____	_____	_____	3. Are volunteered for church jobs without first consulting with them.
_____	_____	_____	4. Are expected to be paragons of virtue in order to prove the quality of the family's spiritual or ministry zeal.
_____	_____	_____	5. Must compete with ministry activities for attention at home.
_____	_____	_____	6. Understand the possibility of conflict or disagreeable situations in ministry activities or among church members.
_____	_____	_____	7. Have seen Christian love, forgiveness, and acceptance practiced regularly at home.

Process your answers by considering the following points. *Yes* answers for questions 1, 6, and 7 show sensitivity to your child's need in relation to your family's ministry role. *Yes* answers on the remaining questions suggest that expectations may be restrictive in some areas. Being in the church or in church activities is not enough to take care of sharing God's grace in the family. Family members need to see redemption at work at home in your relationship to them.

Responding to Criticism and Conflict

Conflict and criticism are normal occurrences in human interaction. People are different and have varied needs, wants, motives, and ways of doing things. When these differences meet head on, discord emerges.

Understanding and applying some positive response techniques can help in handling unpleasant encounters. The guidelines suggested here are aimed more at family or informal relationships. However, the approaches may often be effective in other areas as well. Check your present coping patterns as you go through these response techniques.

Handling Criticism

Criticism can reflect several motives on the

part of a critic. First, *criticism can be based on a valid complaint*. The motive here is straightforward—an injury needs to be acknowledged and mended. Second, *criticism may be used to motivate behavior in a desired direction*. Here the motive may be sincere but misguided. Criticism usually results more in guilt and avoidance than in compliance. Third, *criticism may result from confusion or misunderstanding*. Dealing with the source of the confusion usually ends the criticism. Finally, *criticism can build self up at another's expense*. The motive in this case reflects the critic's sense of low esteem, and no real basis need exist for the complaint.

Several steps can be taken in responding to criticism:

• *Hear the critic out*. Your attention may take some of the negative fears out of the situation. Listening also encourages the critic to express feelings openly. As you listen you may discover the underlying cause of the criticism.

• *Listen to the message implied in the criticism.* Try to separate the gist of the complaint from the words used. Is the complaint justified, or is it actually a put-down or manipulation attempt? Has the critic chosen you as the handiest target for his or her irritation at some other problem? Could the critic be reacting out of envy or low self-esteem? If you do not hear any actual wrongdoing on your part, forget the criticism and concentrate on helping the critic.

• *Resist defensiveness or replying in kind*. Realize that it is possible for others to interpret your behavior in ways contrary to your intention. Inwardly affirm your own worth so you can feel secure in hearing the truth about yourself or in coping with put-downs. Seeing that you are not crushed by the criticism may disarm the critic. If the critic is sincere, the problem can be worked through appropriately. If the critic is out to manipulate you, the ploy will be out in the open and largely robbed of effect.

• *Respond positively to the critic*.[3] Acknowledge your error when at fault, "You're right. That was not the thing to do." Your acceptance of responsibility cools the attack and affirms both your worth and that of the critic. The relationship will be improved and communication eased.

If the critic is insincere or the criticism unjustified, a positive response can still prove helpful. You might reply, "I can see that you are upset by this," or "I hadn't looked at it from that angle before." You might ask for more detail, "I don't understand what made you feel this way." Such responses are non-critical of the other person. Usually the critic will clarify his or her feelings or realize you will not be manipulated. If the critic thinks irrationally, arguing will not prove or settle anything. The writer of Proverbs surely had a positive response in mind, "A gentle answer quiets anger, but a harsh one stirs it up" (15:1).

Handling Conflict Situations

Conflict is sometimes painful, but it need not be considered unhealthy or harmful if handled redemptively. Many of the same approaches to handling criticism also apply in dealing with conflict. Accept the possibility of controversy. Assure family members they can express feelings and opinions openly. Such expressions do not have to be agreed with or approved of, but they do need to be heard. Encourage them to state their disagreement as soon as possible rather than brooding over it until a major breakdown in relationship occurs.

Hearing the conflict in a calm way calls for some specific ground rules:

1. *Identify the cause of the conflict*. Try to nail down the point of disagreement as clearly as possible: differing opinions, methods, or goals. What behavior sparked the fuss?

2. *Focus on behavior rather than people*. Such focus is less threatening to parties in the dispute. For example, one child complains, "John is messy. He can't do anything right. He's ruining our room." Shift focus from John to his actions, "Working on the science project has messed up the bedroom." Behavior, opinions, or goals can be changed; they are more impersonal or neutral in nature. However, focusing on the person is perceived as an attack on self-esteem. The person is more likely to react defensively and fail to work through the issue cooperatively.

3. *Hear all sides of the issue*. Encourage all parties to speak, and insist that they hear each other out before replying.

4. *Keep discussion centered on the issue at hand*. Don't tell past disagreements, failures, or actions. Don't drag in other problems which may confuse the matter at hand.

5. *Underscore points of agreement*. As in the

example of John and the science project, certain things did take place that both sides can agree on: John needs to complete the project and working on it is messy.

6. *Find possible solutions.* Ask for suggestions from all parties. What options are available? Is a compromise possible? For example, could John work on his project in the garage? If not, could he work in a small area and minimize mess by working over old newspapers or the like?

7. *Agree to carry out the solution.* Settle who will do what and when. If no solution is possible, agree on what will take place: drop the subject, discuss it later, or reopen discussion if new options come up. The main thing is to avoid drawing the conflict out. Often the act of airing grievances or learning another's reasoning can change the situation. Even if no solution is possible, all parties should feel affirmed in having had their say.

Affirming personal worth is very important in facing both criticism and conflict. Understanding and accepting another's feelings make you more apt to respond rather than merely react. Positive self-esteem enables you to deal with valid criticism without becoming defensive. In conflict situations high self-esteem allows you to concede points, negotiate solutions, and work toward resolution without loss of self-worth. Sure of your own personhood, you can take a more balanced view of the issue. Your self-worth gains strength from a vital source in peacemaking,

"Your life in Christ makes you strong, and his love comforts you. You have fellowship with the Spirit, and you have kindness and compassion for one another" (Phil. 2:1).

Underscoring Family Strengths

Look at your family life in the context of ministry. Help your children understand the pressures that may come from this environment. Help them respond appropriately to expectations. Be yourself and allow your children to be themselves. Affirm each other's unique personality, gifts, and capacities so that unrealistic ideals have minimal impact.

Let your children know when a conflict situation has come up in your ministry situation.[4] Children may not understand the issue and fear something terrible will happen to the family. Explain the problem in terms suitable to a child's age. For a small child you might say, "Some people don't agree with what Daddy is doing. So, if you hear some unhappy things, you will know what is going on. We are trying to do the right thing. God loves us, and whatever happens we will be together and work it out." This kind of assurance helps a child deal with very real fears in a sensible way.

Help your children understand also the joys and benefits of ministry as well as the pressures. There is much to recommend a vocation which works toward mending brokenness in peoples' lives and shares the good news of God's love.

Reflection

1. People of faith are called *God's family* (1 John 3:1). God is often described like a parent in relation to his people (Ps. 103:13). What attributes of God in dealing with his family might you use in nurturing yours?

2. Which of God's attributes as Father do you feel you need most right now as his child?

6

Building Support

Help carry one another's burdens, and in this way you will obey the law of Christ (Gal. 6:2).

Joan stared after the moving van as it pulled out of the driveway. Watching family belongings on the way to a new home made her feel very empty and lonely. Joan's husband had served a church in town for eight years. Two children were born during this time, and the oldest child could recall no other home. The new church lay three states away, almost a thousand miles from both sets of in-laws, and in a totally different kind of community. For the first time since seminary days, Joan felt cut off from everything and everyone dear to her.

Joan's feelings are not unusual ones. Anyone leaving well-established friendships, familiar surroundings, and comfortable routines goes through this sense of loss. Disruption in personal support systems triggers anxiety and loneliness.

You may assume your life is pretty stable and support is automatic until facing a crisis. At such times you reach out for assurance, encouragement, and counsel from those you hold dear. You feel vulnerable without such reinforcement.

Support, however, is not automatic, nor is it accidental. Good support systems are built and sustained like other important relationships in life. Crisis brings support to the forefront more acutely, but the need exists every day. You will want to tap this vital resource for yourself and your family.

Identifying Support Needs

All families need undergirding in the areas of affirmation, acceptance, and accountability. But ministry families are especially vulnerable if they cannot find such assurance in their responsibilities.

When asked to name their most real problems, one group of ministers' wives put "few close friends" at the top of their list.[1] Over 70 percent of the group agreed they had many acquaintances but few real friends. Further, 60 percent of the wives chose not to form close friendships within their husband's ministry setting. These concerns seem to be fairly typical of many ministers' wives. The situation often produces a sense of deep loneliness or isolation.

Loneliness in ministry shows up on surveys so often that it can almost be considered an occupational hazard. The nature of ministry, its symbolic overtones, and its public role, tend to work against very close relationships in a local church setting. Those working in fields of ministry outside a local congregation also experience similar feelings. Peer support may be lacking due to service responsibilities, work locale, or competitiveness between individuals or agencies. Vocational demands often include long hours of travel, study, and meetings which limit relationships to casual encounters or business discussions. Time at home with the family is limited as well.

A major part of loneliness for ministry families stems from leadership roles they assume.[2] Subtle psychological factors intrude into relationships between those who lead and those who follow. Relating to large numbers of people in mostly formal settings tends to put distance between ministry families and their church associates. Little opportunity for personal disclosure or mutual understanding takes place.

The ministry setting, then, calls for a support system that provides openness, acceptance, and understanding. Most of all, ministry families need a support environment where they can relate as equals to others, be themselves, and put aside the leadership role for a time.

Assess your support needs by completing the following survey. Circle the number that best describes your situation:

5 = very satisfactory				1 = very unsatisfactory	
5	4	3	2	1	Close friends within your local church membership.
5	4	3	2	1	Close friends outside your local church membership.

5	4	3	2	1	Friendship with other ministry couples nearby.
5	4	3	2	1	Close relationships with relatives of self or spouse.
5	4	3	2	1	Travel distance to visit relatives.
5	4	3	2	1	Travel distance to visit best friends.
5	4	3	2	1	Opportunity for relating to others outside your ministry leadership role.
5	4	3	2	1	Children's relationship with their age groups in the church.
5	4	3	2	1	Children's relationship with their age groups in school or neighborhood.
5	4	3	2	1	Opportunity for social outings with persons of similar interests as self.
5	4	3	2	1	Opportunity to share problems, concerns confidentially with other ministry couples.
5	4	3	2	1	Opportunity to share problems, concerns with other ministers' wives.
5	4	3	2	1	Assistance available in family crisis (illness, injury, death).
5	4	3	2	1	Assistance available in church conflict situation or job loss.

Review your answers. Which areas received the lowest rating? Do you sense a need for more support in these low areas? Which areas of support need to be built or strengthened? Keep your assessment in mind as you go through this chapter. Look for options you might use in building or improving your personal support system.

Most ministers and their wives see each other as their main support persons. While this kind of support is crucial, no couple can meet all support needs within themselves. Gaining support from a wider group is essential. Consider now some of the ways you might extend your support network.

Kinds of Support

Support needs can be summarized in three major categories: primary support, social support, and growth support. *Primary support* involves helping you survive day by day. Nurture, protection, and crisis care are largely met at this level. *Social support* refers to peer relationships and outlets for personal expression through recreation or shared interests. *Growth support* comes from individuals or groups who provide encouragement and accountability in personal development. This area moves beyond social activity to a deeper level of sharing.

Let's examine each of these support areas. Review each of the areas in terms of your support needs.

Primary Support

Survival, maintainance, or daily nurture describe primary support. This basic type of care comes from those close to you in day-to-day situations. You probably have in mind a number of persons you feel free to call on for help, encouragement, or problem solving. Family, friends, neighbors, and church associates are logical persons to include in this type of support network.

Check the possibilities for your primary support system by filling in the following lists. Name persons in the various groups you can look to for help, encouragement, or practical guidance:

1. My present household: _____

_____

2. My close relatives: _____

_____

_____

3. My husband's family: _____

_____

_____

4. Close friends nearby: _____

_____

_____

5. Neighbors: _____

_____

_____

6. Church fellowship: _____

_____

_____

Review your answers with these questions in mind: Which persons have the closest relationship with you? Which persons offered help in the past? Which persons have you asked for help? Which persons continually give you the most encouragement and affirmation? Do you need to strengthen relationships with any of those listed? Have you expressed your concern and support to those listed?

Examine the kind of support you expect from those listed in the primary support groups. Name persons you would feel free to call on for help in the following situations:

Illness or injury to self: _____

Illness or injury to spouse or child: _____

Death in the family: _____

Financial problem: _____

Job loss: _____

Emergency child care: _____

Personal loneliness: _____

Recreation or relaxation: _____

Personal problem: _____

Help in completing a task: _____

Some primary support needs to come from community professionals or helping groups.

List persons you can rely on in these areas:

Medical Care:
  Self _____
  Spouse _____
  Child _____
Dental Care: _____
Legal Advice: _____
Financial Guidance:
  Money management _____
  Investment or purchase _____
  Loan _____
Counseling:
  Personal _____
  Child _____
  Marital _____

Spiritual _____
Career Guidance: _____

If you have not established contact with professionals in these areas, consider doing so. Who can you ask for reliable referrals? What sources of information on helping professionals or groups are available to you? What resources does your denomination or ministry agency provide in these areas?

Support systems can be found within the local church for ministry families in that vocational setting. Coming to a new church field is an ideal time to begin a support system for both ministry and social needs. Initial support can be found in the search committee or official group who recommended your husband to the church. Having recommended him to the congregation, they have a vested interest in seeing your family well received in the community. Church leaders and their families may ease your way into the life of the congregation by explaining customs, making introductions, and giving practical help in finding your way around. If the church has other staff ministers, their families could help with information about shopping, schools, community facilities, and the like. Church age groups can be the first contact persons for new social outlets.

Maintaining an active primary support system cushions the ups and downs in daily life. Stability and continuity flow from a network of persons who provide concern and care. You will want to reach out to persons who can share primary support with you and your family.

Social Support

Peer relationships exist when persons interact as equals. Neither party to the relationship feels obligated to assume a leadership role. Mutual interest and concern form the basis for this type of support.

Persons or families who share similar interests, hobbies, or age groupings with your family are logical choices for this level of support. Sources of social outlets might be found in parents of your children's friends, local ministry couples, civic or club memberships, and business contacts.

Relief from leadership status might mean excluding church members from this support level, depending on the type of relationship you wish to establish. Ministers and their wives sometimes fear what might happen if they appear to be closer to some church members than others. You will need to evalute your own needs and situation in this regard.

Two-clergy families benefit from relationships with nonclergy families. They do not have to "talk shop" all the time. Their children also need adult role models outside ministry vocations.[3] Extending your social outlets beyond ministry associates will also give a broader perspective on community issues, resources, and concerns. Carry-over will be felt in ministry as well from this wider outlook on community life.

Examine the possibilities for social outlets by filling in the following lists. Name persons or groups who might serve social needs in the following areas:

Parents of children's friends: _____
_____

Local ministry couples of same or other denomination: _____
_____

Professional, civic, or other club members: _____
_____

PTA, school, or athletic group associates of family: _____
_____

Hobby or interest groups: _____

_____

Community professionals outside ministry: _____

_____

Community art, music, or cultural activity groups: _____

_____

Social outlets encourage personal expression and release of pent-up tension. Interaction with a variety of people helps ease depression, loneliness, and self-centeredness. Poise, self-confidence, and self-esteem can be enhanced. Since these benefits answer some of the expressed needs of many ministry couples, you will want to plan a social support system as part of your family's growth concerns.

Growth Support

Growth support helps you reach your potential as a person. Growth support can be short-term or long-term. Marriage enrichment retreats, skill development seminars, spiritual life conferences, and other personal development groups are typical short-term processes. Long-term growth involves sustained participation with others of like concerns. Growth support persons show acceptance, care, and affirmation, but they also challenge you to reach toward your best.

Long-term growth support comes most readily in a group organized for that purpose. Such a group has different purposes than social or primary care groups. Growth support asks for self-disclosure, feedback, and accountability from participants. Group members covenant to help each other deal with issues at a deep level of sharing.

Assess your need for or interest in a growth support group by marking the following statements. Circle the number which best describes your feeling:

		5 = desire very much			1 = don't desire at all
5	4	3	2	1	Acceptance of who I am apart from my role or other external status.
5	4	3	2	1	An atmosphere in which I can be myself.
5	4	3	2	1	Persons who will be completely frank with me.
5	4	3	2	1	Feedback as to how I come across as a person.
5	4	3	2	1	Opportunity to express openly how I feel.
5	4	3	2	1	Help in dealing with my concerns as a minister's wife.
5	4	3	2	1	Understanding by others of the kind of person I really am.
5	4	3	2	1	Freedom to express anger, hurt, or disappointment.
5	4	3	2	1	Opportunity to deal with depression, loneliness or feelings of inadequacy as a minister's wife.
5	4	3	2	1	Motivation to do what I am competent to do.
5	4	3	2	1	Affirmation of my worth and integrity as a person.
5	4	3	2	1	Accountability for reaching toward my growth goals.
5	4	3	2	1	Affirmation of my gifts.
5	4	3	2	1	Sharing in a growth process with others.

Process your answers by considering these questions: Which areas received the highest rankings? Do you now have these needs met through a support system? Do you help meet these needs for persons who share the same concerns? Would a sustained group process help meet your needs in these areas?

If you feel the need for help in dealing with some specific growth issues, you might consider developing or joining a support group. A support group can provide a safe, caring place where you can come to terms with who you are and what you want to see happen in your life.

Developing a Growth Support System

Steps in beginning a growth support group are quite simple but require careful consideration. Begin by deciding what you would like to see happen in a growth group. You might review needs checked in the preceding exercise. Determine some general aim or focus for growth support: dealing with issues you face as a ministers' wife, sharing ways of enhancing family life, time management, skill improvement in communication or interpersonal relationships, learning new parenting approaches, support in simplifying lifestyle, or some interest you would like to explore in a group setting.

Consider persons you'd like to join with you in dealing with these concerns. One possibility might be in identifying other ministers' wives who share similar concerns. You might choose from the community at large: women of similar age, interests, or goals. If you can't find any interest in forming a group, check for an ongoing group which you might join.

Major considerations in forming a group are understanding support group principles, preparing to organize the group, inviting members, and working out the group structure. A brief description of these steps may help you bring your support system into operation.

Group Support Principles

An effective growth support group hinges on certain basic assumptions about sharing together. A different approach is required for growth support than for ordinary social groups. Necessary elements of growth support are:

• *Self-disclosure.* Participants need to be willing to invest themselves openly in sharing. Expressing feelings and concerns must go beyond a surface level. Openness, frankness, and acceptance are crucial to the process. Group members both give of themselves and receive others' concerns in trust.

• *Confidentiality.* Freedom in self-disclosure calls for integrity in keeping concerns within the group. If trust and respect cannot be felt, participants will commit no more to the process than to any gabfest. You risk becoming vulnerable to others in openness, but such trust provides the climate for real growth.

• *Feedback.* Personal assessment takes place more accurately when reflections of self are received from others. Feedback involves expressing perceptions about others' behavior and its effect. Group members help each other see how they come across through speech, actions, and attitudes by honestly describing such behavior.

• *Confrontation.* Challenging or motivating you to take an honest look at yourself is an expression of concern for you. Support group members should care enough about each other to confront. Helping someone confront growth issues can be risky. Lack of acceptance or even rejection may result. However, confrontation is essential to motivate realistic self-examination.

• *Accountability.* Accountability calls for responsibility in chosen growth areas. Support group members or the group as a whole should be able to help you become accountable for growth and reaching toward goals. However, you must ask for such help. You will want to decide whom to ask and what kind of help you need from these persons.

• *Commitment.* Group members need to be willing to invest time and energy to the support process. Meaningful sharing requires building trust through regular attendance and active participation at sessions. Casual interest or haphazard attendance reduces the group to little more than a social outlet.

Make a list of persons who would likely accept the principles of a support group and who share your interests. Contact them about the possibility of starting a growth support group. Explain your concerns and invite them to discuss their interest in a group. Set a time and place to meet for this exchange of ideas.

Support Group Preparation

The first meeting of persons interested in a growth support group will lay the foundation for the group and its future direction. If you are getting the group together, your preparation can pave the way for better understanding of the process.

Gather some materials to help familiarize you with the work of support groups. Guidebooks and cassette tapes are available which explain the nature and organization of support systems. Howard J. Clinebell's *People Dynamic: Changing Self and Society Through Growth Groups* (New York: Harper and Row) is a resource on understanding the group process. A cassette tape series by Duane Meyer (Minneapolis: Ministers Life Resources) deals with professional group support for clergy, but the principles apply to any group. If you will be leading the meeting, be prepared to share information about support groups.

You might wish to have a facilitator or support group trainer attend the initial meeting. Facilitators may be available from a local counseling center, university, denominational agency, or nearby support group. The facilitator's task will be to focus the group's thinking, help set up the group organization, and assist in working out an agenda. The facilitator will not do the group's work, only lend expertise in starting the group. The group must make its own decisions and choose to sustain its own existence.

Organization Steps

The initial meeting assesses interests of those attending. If individuals show interest in forming a group, some guidelines are set up to direct future sessions. Activities move along lines similar to these:[4]

1. *Introduction.* Individuals introduce themselves if they are not acquainted. The meeting's purpose can be highlighted by asking participants to state why they decided to come to the meeting or what they hope to get out of a support group. After everyone responds, explain the purpose of the meeting and what needs to be accomplished in the rest of the session.

2. *Common interest.* Participants should be asked to suggest topics, concerns, or interests they wish to explore as a group. Once the list has been finished, participants try to narrow it down to items that most interest the group. If enough common interest is found, a group can be formed and a common focus can be decided as the group's purpose.

3. *Meetings.* A regular meeting time and place needs to be set by members. Groups meet often enough to serve needs: weekly, twice a month, monthly, or whatever interval seems practical. A regular meeting place is also convenient if it can be arranged. Members also need to commit themselves to attend regularly.

4. *Format.* The group will want to decide how future sessions will be led. Groups commonly rotate responsibility for each session's design and theme among the members; choose a set agenda to be used at all meetings, or combine elements of these two formats. Beginning groups may benefit from a set agenda. Later sessions may move to other formats as the group develops its own character.

5. *Task assignment.* Responsibility for all tasks needed in carrying out the next meeting should be set. Planning the general direction of the first few meetings would be helpful. Some groups enjoy using the first few meetings to get better acquainted, build trust, and develop support skills. Time needed for reaching a high level of openness varies with each group and the personalities of members.

Sustaining the Support Group

The group's progress and effectiveness should be evaluated periodically. Around the fourth session an evaluation time should be included for one session. Individual members assess whether they are getting what they wanted or expected out of the group. The group as a whole determines feelings about what they are doing. Problems can be faced or changes made in the direction of the group.

The original focus of the group also needs evaluating from time to time. Group interests may shift as the sessions progress. Plans may need to be made for improving or restructuring the group. Meeting time or place may need adjusting.

Decisions about inviting guests or seeking new members will arise. Visitors may bring new interest in the group, but they also break the established closeness of the group. A time of transition will be needed for group adjustment if new members are brought in.

A time limit might be set on the group's existence. Some groups plan a year's sessions and then disband, or some groups intend to be an ongoing process. If so, membership may change as participants drop out. Taking a positive outlook on loss is necessary. A planned exit time might ease departure. The regular evaluation sessions prove appropriate in most groups for celebrating a departing member's contribution to the group.

Consider your interest in forming a support group by answering the following questions:

1. I can benefit from a growth support group because _____
_____
_____

2. The major issues I'd like to focus on in the group are: _____
_____
_____
_____

3. Persons who may share my concerns are: _____
_____
_____
_____
_____

4. A convenient meeting time for me would be on:
_____ (day of the week) at _____ o'clock.
I'd prefer to meet ☐ weekly   ☐ biweekly   ☐ monthly
☐ other: _____
Meetings should last about _____ hours.
Child care ☐ would ☐ would not be needed for me.

5. Persons and resources to help in starting a support group are: _____
_____
_____
_____
_____

A growth support group can be a rewarding experience. You do not have to be professionally trained to form a group. Some knowledge of the group process, willingness to abide by some basic rules, openness and acceptance in sharing, and concern for member's growth will create a support climate.

Support Through Feedback

Support group settings are only one useful arena for feedback. Expressing your perceptions about behavior is an ordinary response: a child misbehaves, your husband asks an opinion of his new ministry project, a young friend wants your reaction to his first sermon, a friend shows off her new hair style—examples are common and almost endless. Making feedback both helpful and supportive is a primary concern.

Some guidelines[5] to use in giving feedback are:

1. *Responding*. Feedback is most effective when asked for rather than volunteered by you. Requests for feedback need to be honored. Failure to respond can create anxiety or doubt about behavior. Too much detail might burden the person, so aim for directness and simplicity.

2. *Timing*. Feedback has more effect the closer it follows the behavior. However, some delay might be helpful if the situation is strained or the person is not really ready to hear it. But too much delay creates uncertainty and may give the impression you are avoiding the person.

3. *Usefulness*. Effective feedback describes only *specific behavior and its effect*: what was said or done and the impact on others. Feedback does not judge the individual's personality or character. Focus is strictly on the action, not on the person. Because useful feedback is descriptive, it is less threatening to the person. For example, a young friend asks your opinion of his first sermon. You might say, "You're a fine young man, and I believe you'll do well once you get some experience." Your reply may be sincere but not particularly helpful. Describing what he did is more useful, "The Scripture and hymns you chose were very appropriate. But I felt you were hurrying through your sermon by speaking so rapidly. I noticed people near the back of

the room were having a hard time hearing." Such descriptive material leaves the person free to use the information or not. You can be candid without appearing judgmental by using good feedback techniques.

4. *Clarity.* You are giving only *your impression* of the behavior. You might encourage the person getting your feedback to check out the feelings of others who also observed the behavior.

5. *Consideration.* Be sensitive to feelings of the one receiving your feedback. Negative feedback can trigger painful feelings. Give the person time to respond. Most people dread hearing negative responses to their behavior. Acknowledge the feelings and assure the hearer of your concern.

Giving useful feedback is a valuable aid in building relationships. Your response can encourage openness in expressing feelings. Appropriate behavior can be reinforced and less desirable action noted with less threat. Further, esteem and confidence in behavior can be affirmed in both yourself and the one receiving the feedback.

Reflection

1. God promises support and care for his people. How have you experienced this promise in your life?

2. What resources has God provided for you which show his support and care?

7

Nurturing Faith

God's divine power has given us everything we need to live a truly religious life through our knowledge of the one who called us to share in his own glory and goodness (2 Pet. 1:3).

Master gardeners plan their planting with great care. They place each flower so that greatest benefit comes from light, moisture, and soil condition. Plants are protected from elements that might crowd out growth. Plants have a natural urge to grow, but growth must be encouraged by providing the best environment possible.

So it is with faith. Deep and active faith does not happen by accident. God's grace enables faith to grow, but growth must be encouraged by choosing the best possible climate for it to take place. This chapter will examine some of the areas which give background to expressing and enhancing faith. Each person's needs and spiritual maturity are different, but some general influences touch most lives.

Compare your nurturing skills as you look again at some everyday aspects of faith.

Barriers to Spiritual Growth

Ministers and their families live in the midst of religious activity. Yet this very attention to matters of religion can produce some barriers to spiritual growth. Some common problem areas are often found in:

• *Time commitment.* Many service tasks are open to you in a church setting. Often needs are great, and you may feel obligated to assume responsibility for many activities. Becoming overcommitted to activities without considering personal time limitations, however, is quite easy. You may feel used up from preparation, attendance, and performance in so many duties. In that case personal life may be dropped to the background of attention. Personal devotional pursuits can be bypassed with inadequate time for reflection and meditation.

• *Public image.* As a minister's wife you are probably expected to pray, give devotionals, and lend a "spiritual" tone to most social or church gatherings you attend. Continually acting out of this public image can strain devotional life if it is not balanced by personal growth opportunites. It is easy to assume that feeding others feeds you as well.

• *Unresolved feelings.* At times you may feel anger, fear, frustration, envy, and other emotions that are often thought sinful for Christians. The idea is sometimes heard that having such feelings implies lack of faith. Guilt may build up if you accept this reasoning. You may be tempted to hide or deny feelings day after day rather than deal with them. These repressed feelings can lie under the surface like raw edges to prayer or worship.

• *Failed expectations.* You may have come to your role as a minister's wife with high ideals of commitment and service. If you've had a typical relationship in your service area, many of these ideals have been battered or possibly crushed. As a result, disappointment with yourself or perhaps with God may have built up.

Another area of failed expectations may come from mistreatment at the hands of church members or other ministry personnel. Ministers and their families sometimes suffer from job termination, conflict situations, gossip, competition for status or recognition, or lack of dignity in living conditions and respect in serving. Such situations often produce a sense of bitterness in serving. God's purpose in mending brokenness becomes blurred in personal pain. Inattention or indifference to devotional life could result.

• *Perfectionism.* Perhaps as a side effect of expectations, a drive to be perfect in everything may arise. This striving may be a defense against criticism or an attempt to meet your or others' unrealistic expectations. But the demand on emotional energy can be tremendous in maintaining this struggle. Each failure or error will become a new source of disappointment in personal worth or service.

• *Unacknowledged humanity.* This attitude simply means not accepting the fact of being a finite, mortal individual. Serving in ministry sometimes gives persons the notion they can break all the rules of physical or emotional care. God is expected to work miracles in taking up the slack left by improper rest, diet, exercise, or emotional release. Depression and isolation can rob devotional life of its joy as a result.

• *Neglected covenants.* The covenant to serve God in ministry can come to be *the only* covenant if care is not taken. But many covenants fill life: marriage, parenthood, friendship, business and social integrity, and community concern. All these covenants fill a place in God's service, and these bonds of responsibility need to be honored once they are made. Authentic servanthood is characterized by wholeness in all of life.

• *Limited vision.* This barrier concerns the tendency to forget that God has a viewpoint on his world. Theologians call limited vision a *lack of transcendence*, a failure to look beyond self to glimpse God at work in his world. Trying to define God's purpose as material success or popularity can limit vision to human levels. But God is greater than we know, beyond narrow human concepts of his power or grace. Faith ever reaches for a wider vision of God's purpose (Eph. 1:18-19).

Perhaps you have felt a tug of familiarity at some of these barriers. Maybe you have identified some of them as your own. That is why it is important to affirm anew that God's grace is at work in you, calling you to spiritual wholeness in him.

Assess your present climate for nurturing faith. Consider the following statements, and respond to them as you feel:

1. For me, faith is hardest when it comes to _____
_____
_____
_____

2. I feel my greatest barriers to spiritual nurture are _____
_____
_____
_____
_____

3. I feel closest to God when I _____
_____
_____
_____
_____

4. I want my faith to be _____
_____
_____
_____

5. I think my devotional life could be strengthened by _____
_____
_____
_____
_____

What barriers have you identified in nurturing faith? How do you feel they affect your approach to daily experience? Do you see any ways of changing or redefining your activities to help in nurturing faith?

Nurturing faith is a very complex, personal issue. One big problem with trying to define ways to do it is that there is *no one-and-only* *approach.* Everyone agrees that nurturing faith is vital to all Christians, essential for those in ministry. But that is the last point of agreement. Methods vary for different people— each is unique in personality, background experiences, spiritual maturity, and pilgrimage of faith. But you can discover spiritual depth in a way that is meaningful for you.

EXPENSE RECORD 19___

REGULAR EXPENSE	JAN	FEB	MAR	APR	MAY	JUN	JUL	AUG	SEP	OCT	NOV	DEC
Taxes												
Life Insurance												
Car Ins., Tags												
Housing												
Utilities												
Food												
Credit Cards												
Tithe												
Transportation												
Personal (cash)												
Medical/Dentist												
Other:												

Spiritual growth is meant to be a practical part of everyday life.

Let's look at four areas where faith comes into contact with daily activities. Consider your approach to these areas. See if options can be found to enrich the climate in which your faith finds nurture and expression.

Simplifying Life-style

Jesus noted the great amount of worry spent on food, clothing, property, and material success (Matt. 6:19-34). Attitudes have not changed since Jesus described the power and influence of possessions. Our culture stresses buying, owning, and using possessions to express worth and identity. Value is attached to new, fashionable clothing, housing, cars, and gadgets. Status symbols are bought to impress others with personal achievement or material success.

Life-style reflects in large part your attitude toward possessions. Mastering the use and meaning of possessions is the handiest means of controlling many daily concerns. Since so much energy and resources go into gaining possessions, you will want to look at your attitude toward them as part of nurturing faith.

Planning the Use of Resources

Financial pressures are not at the top of the list of concerns expressed by ministers' wives. Issues such as time use, expectations, conflict situations, ministry demands, moving, and handling criticism rank higher.[1] Yet finances are a concern for most families, and managing resources is often both a challenge and a struggle.

One way to cope with financial demands is to anticipate and plan spending. Have you ever kept a record of where your family income goes in a year? The answers are sometimes surprising and always revealing. Family priorities readily surface on check stubs and receipts.

If you do not have an accurate idea of regular expenses, try keeping the expense record shown on page 62 for one year. The chart can be drawn on a larger piece of paper if more space is needed. Two pieces of lined notebook paper glued or taped together make an inexpensive but handy record form. The chart simply provides space for regular expense amounts to be listed by the month. Categories shown are samples of typical expenses. You may need to adjust your chart to reflect your own expense categories. Make the record as detailed as needed to be helpful.

Large expenditures occurring only periodically (taxes and insurance, for example) can be anticipated ahead of time by coloring their chart block with a marker pen or transparent marker. When a rather large expense is due the next month, you can adjust current spending to ease the extra outlay. Recording regular expenses for one year will enable you to estimate income needs more accurately. Once needs are clearly in mind, you can plan a budget to manage use of income.

Get an overall picture of your family's financial condition. Determine assets and liabilities. Is a regular savings plan in force? Is retirement income being provided? Can health or financial emergencies be handled reasonably well? For example, what kind of strain would the budget suffer by replacing the car or a major appliance? What expenses could be cut if income were unexpectedly cut $200 or more per month?

Try to decide some family priorities in spending. Set reasonable limits on purchases and stick by them. Get feedback from family members on using undesignated funds. Help your children understand the limits and uses of family resources.

Take into account your valid needs in life-style when setting limits on spending. There is no virtue in false economy. Rigorous self-denial may not be the answer to a proper regard for possessions. Hang-ups can come over very little as easily as over much when it comes to possessions.

Deciding the Meaning of Possessions

Financial pressures exert subtle but powerful influence. Advertising presents many items that are purely status symbols. Certain name brands may represent prestige or power in fashion trends. Children, especially teens, face considerable peer pressure in having just the "right" things. Status trends are potent forces in choices about spending.

Acquiring a certain level of material goods can be the primary goal of getting an income. Families often commit themselves to a particular life-style without first considering its benefits or costs. If two incomes are needed to buy status items, then energy will be invested to that end. Before committing to a certain life-style, you might want to examine its fulfillment potential for family members. You also might want to examine motives in choosing that life-style. Count the costs in terms of physical, mental, and emotional demands. Ask yourself: Will the house, car, or other possessions own me?

Self-esteem is often reflected in how resources are used. Parents sometimes feel inadequate when they cannot supply children with "nice things" others may have. Credit buying seems the answer to this felt inadequacy. Yet credit buying only puts more pressure on parents. Anxieties build about debts and possible job loss. Take a careful look at how possessions relate to your feelings of self-esteem.

Your ministry situation may place you in relationship with persons whose income is greater than your own. Pressure may be felt to match their life-styles. Try to consider your worth in serving and your valid needs before investing resources in this kind of pursuit.

Check your family's attitude toward possessions by checking the following statements. Circle the number that most nearly describes your feeling:

5 = always

3 = sometimes

4 = usually

2 = rarely

1 = never

5	4	3	2	1	Value is stressed in purchases rather than status.
5	4	3	2	1	Our family understands basic advertising techniques and their buying pressure on people.
5	4	3	2	1	We wait to see if something is really needed before buying it.
5	4	3	2	1	We enjoy things without owning them (public parks, museums, library facilities).
5	4	3	2	1	Our children are allowed to experience the consequences of unwise choices in spending.
5	4	3	2	1	Possessions are not tests of happiness, success, or fulfillment for us.
5	4	3	2	1	We try to practice and teach making good decisions in purchases.
5	4	3	2	1	We enjoy activities together that have little or no cost (walking, biking, games, backyard outings).
5	4	3	2	1	Stewardship of material and natural resources is part of our life-style.

Which areas ranked lowest in your answers? Do priorities need to be examined in these areas? Much pressure can be removed from family decisions by resolving the role of possessions. Realize that you don't have to buy everything that is advertised in order to have a rich, full life. As simple as this sounds, it is a major decision. Too often family expenses relate more to media pressure than to actual needs.

Resisting impulse buying and status purchases can free up both resources and attitudes for more vital concerns in family relationships.

Setting Priorities

Priorities are those things which hold the most significance for you. They reflect much of your goals and direction in life. Time, resources, and energy are spent on priority activities. Selecting something as a priority means you value it very highly. You declare through such choices, "This is really important to me."

To focus on your priorities, fill in the following exercise. First, list on the lines ten activities that you consider priorities in your life—things you most enjoy and feel to be essential:

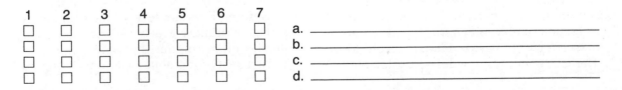

1	2	3	4	5	6	7	
☐	☐	☐	☐	☐	☐	☐	a. _____
☐	☐	☐	☐	☐	☐	☐	b. _____
☐	☐	☐	☐	☐	☐	☐	c. _____
☐	☐	☐	☐	☐	☐	☐	d. _____

☐ ☐ ☐ ☐ ☐ ☐ ☐ e. _____

☐ ☐ ☐ ☐ ☐ ☐ ☐ f. _____

☐ ☐ ☐ ☐ ☐ ☐ ☐ g. _____

☐ ☐ ☐ ☐ ☐ ☐ ☐ h. _____

☐ ☐ ☐ ☐ ☐ ☐ ☐ i. _____

☐ ☐ ☐ ☐ ☐ ☐ ☐ j. _____

Process your answers by testing each item with the following statements.[2] If the priority item listed meets the test of a statement, place a check √ in the appropriate box to the left of the item. Review each priority by all seven tests.

1. I choose to do this item over other activities that are options at the same time.
2. I am willing to invest money, time, and energy in this activity.
3. I carry out this activity regularly, at least weekly.
4. I show concern for this activity by planning, preparing, or learning more about it.
5. I enjoy telling others about this activity.
6. I get a sense of fulfillment or pleasure from this activity.
7. I have grown as a person through this activity.

Did any items receive check marks from all seven tests? If so, they rank as very important to you. Which items appear on the list as your highest priorities (those receiving the most check marks)? You might use the tests to rank other activities not listed in the exercise. This exercise may give you some clues to choices you make in daily activities.

You might also wish to expand your concept of priorities by considering how you choose what is important to you. What standards or tests do you apply in setting priorities? What goals do you have in mind in planning your choices? Your choices reveal your interests, feelings, beliefs, goals, attitudes, and direction in life. Even when events are forced on you, some choice remains in how you respond. Do you need to redefine your priorities or standards for choosing them? How can you set priorities so that your important beliefs and goals are realized?

Deepening Devotional Life

Deepening devotional life calls for opening up all of your day to God's presence. God is there, but recognition of his presence needs to be made more specific as you go through activities. Examine for a moment some of the methods which help build your awareness of spiritual resources.

Solitude

Try setting aside some portion of each day for a time of solitude and silence. Clear your mind and heart of distractions. Solitude is not the aim of Christian life or the primary activity in serving; but it is a valuable tool in helping you find spiritual strength. Solitude can deepen your sensitivity to God's presence in daily happenings.

Look for ways to build a time of solitude into your regular routine. Driving, walking, or performing some extended activity can be used if you can discipline your thinking. Or, choose a time when other activities will not intrude. The idea is to still the clatter of daily demands for a time to let deep concerns of the spirit surface.

Listening Prayer

Much prayer activity involves praise, thanksgiving, confession, requests, or intercession. These are vital concerns in prayer. But you will also find strength in prayer that listens rather than speaks. Give God the gift of your quietness. Allow his Spirit to touch the deepest levels of your being.

The listening prayer is much like tuning a radio to receive the broadcast signal. Heart and mind grow more sensitive to what God is revealing of himself, his will, and his grace.

Reflective Bible Study

Use some time for reflective Bible study. This type of study does not center around preparing to teach a text, defining word meaning, or taking a particular stance. It simply means reading a text and letting the words speak to your needs at that moment. Some people read from the Psalms or some familiar passage for this purpose each day.

The idea in reflective study is to approach

God's Word with an open mind and heart. Like the listening prayer, reflective study is an act of receiving wisdom, grace, peace, comfort, or understanding from allowing God's revelation to reach into your present situation.

Expanded Worship

If you take a leadership role in worship services (choir member, accompanist, or the like), you may be concentrating on performance as much as personal worship. Try opening up each worship activity to God's presence in you. This does not mean stopping all activity or dropping your responsibilities. Rather, fill each activity with awareness of God's leading. Listen for what God may be saying to you through prayers, music, sermon, Scripture, or responses of fellow worshipers. Seeking God's presence in worship activities can help eliminate distractions and bring added meaning to your participation. Jesus assured believers that seeking after God would be rewarded with his presence (Luke 11:9).

Solitude, listening prayer, reflective Bible study, and expanded worship all have one thing in common: concentrating on how God is coming to you through others, events, Scripture, surroundings, awareness, and so on. Opening up your life to God helps put self in perspective with the world around you. This in turn puts a redemptive light on the way you see both yourself and others. You may realize more fully God's power at work in and through you to do his will.

Affirming Spiritual Gifts

Affirming spiritual gifts involves accepting yourself as the person God created you to be—the unique blend of traits, capacities, and personality that you are. God has called you his own, provided redemption, and offered his grace. As his child you are his gift to the church and his redemptive instrument in the world. You have a place in his purpose that calls forth the gifts you possess (1 Cor. 12:4-7).

Affirming your gifts requires two kinds of insight. First, you have some sense of what God leads you to do. Second, fellow believers will affirm what they sense your gifts to be. God works through both insights to guide you.

Focus on your gifts by filling in these statements:

1. I sense gifting in these areas _____

2. I succeed at and enjoy using these abilities and skills _____

3. Others have affirmed these gifts in me _____

4. The gifts others most often call on me to use are _____

Review your answers by considering these questions: Do others see your gifts in the same way as you do? Do others appear hesitant or reluctant in accepting your perception of your gifts? What does this mean in identifying your gifts? Have you discussed your insight into your gifts with someone whose spiritual wisdom you respect and trust? How can you affirm your gifts through serving?

The New Testament lists over twenty kinds of spiritual gifts ranging all the way from simple hospitality to generosity in giving to preaching and teaching (Rom. 12:6-8; 1 Cor. 12:4-10,28-30; Eph. 4:11; 1 Pet. 4:10-11). These are not all the possible gifts needed by the church or in serving. Gifts are called forth as needs arise. Your gift enables you to share in the life and work of God's people. As provider of your gifts, God will help you affirm and use them through his Spirit.

Reflection

1. What choices can you make about daily activities and life-style that will help nurture your faith?

2. What resources has God provided to help you deepen and strengthen your life in him?

8

Putting It All Together

Instead, your beauty should consist of your true inner self, the ageless beauty of a gentle and quiet spirit, which is of the greatest value in God's sight (1 Pet. 3:4).

Traditional ideas about a woman's life began to undergo testing and challenge in the past decade. Conflicting claims and goals grew from new expectations of women. Focus of women's attention shifted from home and family to career and economic independence.

The result of these shifts in attitude has been both positive and negative. Women have been challenged to realize self-fulfillment and personal growth. At the same time, anxiety has come from conflicting expectations. Women have been left to juggle demands of home, career, husband, children, church and community concerns, and personal ideals without much in the way of direction. Few practical guidelines have emerged to help women assess their growth needs.

Dissatisfaction has often been the end product of adopting well-publicized current goals for women without considering their impact on personal growth or potential. All women are not cut out to pursue the same paths to self-fulfillment. The purpose of activities in this book has been to help focus on your identity as a person. Growth issues such as self-esteem, expectations, feelings, communicating, family pressures, support needs, and personal faith have been examined. You will want to establish your self-concept on a firm foundation—the reality of who you are. Your best direction lies in knowing who you are and who you can become in Christian maturity.

You can choose your own growth goals and what you wish to do about them in the future. Growth is intentional, not accidental. Reaching toward your potential means assessing needs, identifying growth areas, setting goals, planning strategies to meet goals, and implementing means to carry them out.

This chapter is designed to help you pull together discoveries about yourself and make redemptive use of them.

Understanding Growth

Growth takes place at a point of need. Areas of concern, weakness, discomfort, restlessness, or uneasiness are potential growth points. Who and what you are creates tension with who and what you can be. But the tension is the first factor leading to growth. Tension gives the first clue to a need. Need gives clues to direction in growth.

Understanding growth may be clearer by noting what it is and is not. *Growth is not changing your real self.* You are born with a set of traits which are uniquely yours. Any attempt to alter or deny these traits will bring only frustration. Second, *growth is not copying someone else's personality.* You may be inspired by others or seek helpful methods in growth, but they cannot provide your inner direction. Finally, *growth is not adopting aggressive individualism.* Self-expression at all costs simply unloads personal issues on others without dealing with them.

By contrast, consider the basic premises of growth. *Growth builds on who you are.* Growth takes direction by discovering and accepting both personal assets and vulnerabilities. These traits are evaluated and compared with what you would like to see happen in your life. Second, *growth involves enhancing and using your own capacities, gifts, and personality.* Finding realistic ways to help reach your potential is the aim of meaningful growth goals. Finally, *growth affirms individuality.* You are a person of God-given worth. Yet this affirmation does not exalt the self at others' expense. Meaningful development as an individual refers to confidence in capabilities, decision making, risk taking, and responsibility for actions. You seek to act out of your personhood rather than dominate others with it.

Growth challenges you to become more of what God created you to be. God's grace provides the strength for self-acceptance and self-understanding. Personal weakness or vulnerability need not be a barrier to growth. Of more importance is your desire to grow and your persistence in moving toward your potential, "because God is always at work in you to make you willing and able to obey his own purpose" (Phil. 2:13).

Elements in Growth Readiness

Readiness for growth involves certain elements which aid the process. Rate your readiness by circling the number that best describes your feeling:

				5 = very good		1 = very poor
5	4	3	2	1	Willing to change—attitude, life-style, behavior.	
5	4	3	2	1	Willing to take an honest look at self and assess both assets and vulnerabilities.	
5	4	3	2	1	Able to accept self and build on who I am.	
5	4	3	2	1	Able to acknowledge, express, and deal with feelings.	
5	4	3	2	1	Willing to confront personal issues and deal with them.	
5	4	3	2	1	Able to accept feedback about self from others.	
5	4	3	2	1	Capable of making decisions about personal needs.	
5	4	3	2	1	Willing to risk taking action once growth goals are set.	
5	4	3	2	1	Willing to evaluate growth and growth goals.	
5	4	3	2	1	Committed to spiritual growth and maturity through personal choice and action.	

Review your answers. Which areas ranked highest? Do these areas show a strong sense of self-esteem? Which areas ranked lowest? Do these areas indicate you may not feel free to be yourself or risk dealing with personal issues? Compare your strong points in growth readiness with areas of need. How can you use these strengths effectively in reaching toward your growth goals?

Getting some idea of your willingness to tackle growth issues can help you focus on areas which create tension for you. Tension can point to areas in which you might like to see change or growth take place. If you are unwilling to acknowledge personal vul-

nerabilities, growth is unlikely to take place. Recognizing need is the first step to identifying growth areas.

Identifying Growth Areas

Review each of the previous chapters, focusing on exercises dealing with different aspects of personhood. As you examine responses, look for areas of concern, tension, or discomfort you noted in completing exercises. You may or may not find concerns in all areas, but do list any area you feel needs attention. List any problem areas in the following spaces:

1. SELF-ESTEEM: _____
_____
_____

2. EXPECTATIONS:
Personal expectations _____
_____
_____

Role expectations _____
_____
_____

Role stress _____
_____
_____

3. FEELINGS: _____
_____
_____

4. COMMUNICATING:
   Speaking _____
   _____
   _____

   Listening _____
   _____
   _____

   Building communication skills _____
   _____
   _____

5. FAMILY PRESSURES:
   Life stage issues _____
   _____
   _____

   Time use _____
   _____
   _____

   Social outlets _____
   _____
   _____

   Handling criticism and conflict _____
   _____
   _____

6. SUPPORT SYSTEM:
   Personal support _____
   _____
   _____

   Growth support _____
   _____
   _____

7. FAITH:
   Simplifying life-style _____
   _____
   _____

   Priorities _____
   _____
   _____

   Devotional life _____
   _____
   _____

   Spiritual gifts _____
   _____
   _____

Perceived needs indicate your growth areas. Identifying growth areas leads to the next step in the process, setting growth goals.

Setting Growth Goals

Setting growth goals moves through three separate steps. Each step helps put goals into perspective and gives you a handle on your growth process.

1. *Identify specific growth needs.* Locate areas of concern or discomfort. Try to define the need as closely as possible. For example, you may feel discomfort in handling feelings. What specific aspect of feelings troubles you—knowing what you feel, accepting feelings, expressing them to others, or allowing others to express feelings? Try to state the type of discomfort as precisely as you can.

2. *Decide the desired outcome.* What changes would you like to see take place in areas of discomfort or tension? What would you like to happen as a result of growth? In other words, compare your present situation with what you wish it to be.

3. *Define growth measurements.* Select some definite signs that will help you measure progress in dealing with concerns. How will you know when growth takes place? How can you evaluate steps in achieving your goals? Suppose your desired outcome is to express feelings freely. What will indicate growth in that area—speaking up, showing emotion, being more open in relationships, or the like?

Select three growth areas which concern you most at this time. Process each concern through the steps given:

GROWTH AREA 1 _____

1. Growth needs: _____
_____
_____
_____

2. Desired outcome: _____
_____
_____
_____

3. Growth measurements: _____
_____
_____
_____

GROWTH AREA 2 _____

1. Growth needs: _____
_____
_____
_____

2. Desired outcome: _____
_____
_____
_____

3. Growth measurements: _____
_____
_____
_____

GROWTH AREA 3 _____

1. Growth needs: _____
_____
_____
_____

2. Desired outcome: _____
_____
_____
_____

3. Growth measurements: _____
_____
_____
_____

The desired outcome in a growth area forms the goal you reach toward. This desired outcome will be the focus of your activity and the aim of growth strategies you plan.

Strategy Sheet
   GROWTH GOAL _____
  I. Obstacles in the way of my goal are: _____
   _____
   _____
   _____

   I can remove or lessen obstacles by: _____
   _____
   _____
   _____
   _____
   _____
   _____

 II. Growth Strategy to meet goal: Completion date:
   _____   _____
   _____   _____
   _____   _____
   _____   _____
   _____   _____
   _____   _____
   _____   _____
   _____   _____
   _____   _____
   _____   _____

   Goal to be reached by _____ (date)
III. Resources needed: _____
   _____
   _____
   _____
   _____
   _____
   _____

 IV. Support persons: Things I will ask of them:
   _____   _____
   _____   _____
   _____
   _____
   _____
   _____
   _____

  V. I will evaluate progress □ daily   □ weekly   □ monthly
   These measurements will help evaluate progress: _____
   _____
   _____
   _____
   _____
   _____
   _____
   _____
   _____

Strategy Sheet
    GROWTH GOAL _____

  I. Obstacles in the way of my goal are: _____
_____
_____
_____
_____

    I can remove or lessen obstacles by: _____
_____
_____
_____
_____
_____
_____

 II. Growth Strategy to meet goal: Completion date:
_____   _____
_____   _____
_____   _____
_____   _____
_____   _____
_____   _____
_____   _____
_____   _____
_____   _____
_____   _____

    Goal to be reached by _____ (date)

III. Resources needed: _____
_____
_____
_____
_____
_____
_____

IV. Support persons: Things I will ask of them:
_____   _____
_____   _____
_____   _____
_____
_____
_____

  V. I will evaluate progress □ daily □ weekly □ monthly
    These measurements will help evaluate progress: _____
_____
_____
_____
_____
_____
_____
_____
_____

Strategy Sheet
   GROWTH GOAL _____
 I. Obstacles in the way of my goal are: _____
_____
_____
_____

   I can remove or lessen obstacles by: _____
_____
_____
_____
_____
_____
_____

II. Growth Strategy to meet goal: Completion date:
_____   _____
_____   _____
_____   _____
_____   _____
_____   _____
_____   _____
_____   _____
_____   _____
_____   _____
_____   _____

   Goal to be reached by _____ (date)
III. Resources needed: _____
_____
_____
_____
_____
_____
_____

IV. Support persons: Things I will ask of them:
_____   _____
_____   _____
_____   _____
_____
_____
_____

 V. I will evaluate progress ☐ daily ☐ weekly ☐ monthly
    These measurements will help evaluate progress: _____
_____
_____
_____
_____
_____
_____
_____
_____
_____
_____

Planning Growth Strategies

Growth strategies are the means of reaching the desired outcome in a growth area. Growth strategies answer the question, "What specific things must I do to reach my goal?"

Several elements are involved in deciding growth strategies. Consider these factors in your planning:

• *Obstacles.* What prevents you from reaching your goal? What difficulties will have to be overcome? What can you do to lessen or remove obstacles? Are there personal barriers to growth? How can you deal with them more effectively?

• *Growth activities.* What specific actions will help achieve your goal? What will you need to do in starting and keeping up the growth process? Will you need information, skill improvement, practice, or the like?

• *Resources.* What will be involved in reaching your goal? How much money, equipment, study materials, energy, and the like will be needed in carrying out growth activities? How much access do you have to these resources? Where can you get help in obtaining needed resources? How conveniently located are resource supplies or help? What assistance can your denomination or ministry agency provide?

• *Support persons.* Who can help you achieve your growth outcome? How can they help you? What specifically will you ask them to do? Who can you depend on for encouragement in your efforts? Who will hold you accountable in striving toward your goal? Who will provide reliable feedback?

• *Time frame.* How much time will be needed to carry out your strategies? What limits will you set on reaching various steps toward your goal? What amount of time will be required to give your strategies a fair test for helpfulness?

• *Evaluation.* What specific steps will be needed in measuring growth? What sign will show progress has taken place? How will you decide when to change or drop an unsuccessful strategy? How will you know when you have reached your goal?

For the Christian, *prayer* is an essential element in planning growth and deciding growth issues. Submitting your concerns to the leadership of the Holy Spirit puts the whole framework of growth into perspective in God's will and purpose. As the psalmist noted, "Give yourself to the Lord;/trust in him, and he will help you" (Ps. 37:5).

Plan specific growth strategies for the three areas of concern you selected on page 71. Three growth strategy sheets are provided for your use (pp. 72-74). Review the elements for deciding strategies as you plan.

These strategy steps can be used for most any area of growth you choose. Decide where you are in your present situation, what you would like to see happen, and plan the steps which will lead to your desired outcome.

Effectiveness as a Minister's Wife

Review your role as a minister's wife. With the elements of growth strategies in mind (p. 75), see if you can discover ways of enhancing your role effectiveness. To focus on this area, complete the following questions:

1. What part of being a minister's wife do you like best? _____
_____

2. What part do you like least? _____
_____

3. What part of being a minister's wife makes the most demands in these areas:
Time _____
Energy _____
Skills _____
Gifts _____
4. In what part of your role do you feel most competent? _____
_____
_____

5. In what part of your role do you feel most vulnerable? _____
_____
_____

6. What can you do about your role to make it:
More interesting _____
_____

More personally satisfying _____
_____

More fulfilling _____
_____

7. What would you like to see happen in your role as a minister's wife? _____
_____
_____

8. What growth strategies can you plan to help bring about your desired outcome? _____
_____
_____
_____
_____
_____

9. Who can provide support and encouragement as you work toward your goal? _____
_____
_____

10. What resources are available to help you? _____
_____
_____

You may not feel you have much choice in what you do as a minister's wife, but response depends on your attitude and decision. Only you can decide to grow. You can make your role more effective by opening up options for yourself that build on your strengths as a person.

The possibility of intellectual, physical, social, and spiritual growth is God's gift to you. Finding deeper meaning and significance in life makes living worthwhile. A sense of well-being and fulfillment accompanies redemptive growth. Even more important, your openness and assurance as a person help others realize the potential of living within the purpose of God.

The result of acting out of your personhood should make you confident in yourself but not content. Always out before you is the direction God leads you "to that oneness in our faith and in our knowledge of the Son of God; we shall become mature people, reaching to the very height of Christ's full stature" (Eph. 4:13).

Reflection

1. "Continue to grow in the grace and knowledge of our Lord and Savior Jesus Christ" (2 Pet. 3:18) is a biblical challenge to personal development. How have you related this area to other growth issues?

2. What resources has God provided to help you grow in his grace and knowledge?

Notes

Chapter 2

1. Stuart Palmer, *Role Stress: How to Handle Everyday Tension* (Englewood Cliffs, NJ: Prentice-Hall, Inc., 1981), p. 6.
2. Ibid., pp. 17-19.
3. Ibid., pp. 16-17.

Chapter 3

1. Louis McBurney, "Dealing with Feelings," seminar, Glorieta Conference Center, July, 1981.
2. Jesse S. Nirenberg, *Getting Through to People* (Englewood Cliffs, NJ: Prentice-Hall, Inc., 1963), p. 47.
3. Jeffrey Schrank, *Feelings: Exploring Inner Space* (New York: Paulist Press, 1973), pp. 34-35.
4. Manuel J. Smith, *When I Say No, I Feel Guilty* (New York: The Dial Press, 1975), pp. 6,14.
5. David D. Burns. *Feeling Good: The New Mood Therapy* (New York: The New American Library, Inc., 1981), pp. 207-208.
6. Schrank, pp. 17-19.
7. Sidney Simon, *Negative Criticism* (Niles, IL: Argus Communications, 1978).
8. Burns, pp. 326-327.
9. Gerald L. Klerman, "The Age of Melancholy," *Psychology Today* (April, 1979), p. 88.
10. Maggie Scarf, "The More Sorrowful Sex," *Psychology Today* (April, 1979), pp. 45,52.

Chapter 4

1. David Mortensen, *Communication: The Study of Human Interaction* (New York: McGraw-Hill Book Company, 1972), p. 13.
2. Mortensen, pp. 7-10,54-55.
3. Reuel L. Howe, *The Miracle of Dialogue* (New York: The Seabury Press, 1963), p. 29.
4. Nirenberg, p. 109.
5. Ibid., pp. 4-10.

6. Gary Collins, *How to Be a People Helper* (Santa Ana, CA: Vision House Publishers, 1976), pp. 46-47.
7. Nirenberg, p. 57.
8. Charles H. Huber, "An Adlerian Approach to Marital Counseling," *Counseling and Human Development* (November, 1981), pp. 6-9.
9. Nirenberg, p. 166.

Chapter 5

1. Kenneth E. Hayes, "Pastors' Wives Survey," Research Project, Sunday School Board of the Southern Baptist Convention (July, 1976), pp. 26-29.
2. Donna Sinclair, *The Pastor's Wife Today* (Nashville: Abingdon Press, 1981), pp. 74-75.
3. Smith, p. 97.
4. Shirley E. Montgomery, "Family Fatigue: Stress in the Minister's Home," *Church Administration* (February, 1982), p. 42.

Chapter 6

1. J. Clifford Tharp, Jr., "The Minister's Family," Research Project, Sunday School Board of the Southern Baptist Convention (September, 1978), p. 10.
2. Wallace Denton, *The Role of the Minister's Wife* (Philadelphia: The Westminster Press, 1962), p. 67.
3. Sinclair, p. 115.
4. Howard Kirschenbaum and Barbara Glasser, *Developing Support Groups* (La Jolla, CA: University Associates, 1978), pp. 21-30.
5. Mortensen, p. 323.

Chapter 7

1. Hayes, p. 26.
2. Maury Smith, *1973 Annual Handbook for Group Facilitators* (La Jolla, CA: University Associations, 1973), p. 203.

Additional References

Chapter 1

Nathaniel Branden, *The Psychology of Self-Esteem* (New York: Bantam Books, 1976).

Louis McBurney, *Every Pastor Needs a Pastor* (Waco: Word Books, 1977).

Felix E. Montgomery, "Understanding Self-Esteem," *Church Administration* (December, 1982), and "Building Personal Self-Esteem," *Church Administration* (January, 1983).

Grady Nutt, *Being Me* (Nashville: Broadman Press, 1971).

Chapter 4

Marjorie Umphrey, *Getting to Know You: A Guide to Communicating* (Irvine, CA: Harvest House Publishers, 1976).

Chapter 5

Betty J. Coble, *The Private Life of the Minister's Wife* (Nashville: Broadman Press, 1981).

Brooks Faulkner, *Stress in the Life of the Minister* (Nashville: Convention Press, 1981).

Louis McBurney, *Families Under Stress* (Waco: Self-Control Systems, Inc., 1981), cassettes 1 and 2.

Chapter 7

Richard J. Foster, *Freedom of Simplicity* (San Francisco: Harper & Row, Publishers, 1981).

E. Glenn Hinson, *The Reaffirmation of Prayer* (Nashville: Broadman Press, 1979).

Wayne E. Oates, *Nurturing Silence in a Noisy Heart* (Garden City, NY: Doubleday & Company, Inc., 1979).

Chapter 8

J. W. Thomas, *Your Personal Growth* (New York: Frederick Fell, Inc., 1971).

Roger Kaufman, *Identifying and Solving Problems: A System Approach* (La Jolla, CA: University Associates, 1976).

Kay Shurden and others, *Women on Pilgrimage* (Nashville: Broadman Press, 1982).